A Hand in Healing

The Power of Expressive Puppetry

Marge Schneider

ISBN-10: 1-5143-8388-8

ISBN-13: 978-1-5143-8388-9

www.expressivepuppetry.com

This book is dedicated to my clients, who taught me to embrace blunt honesty and relax into silence without having to fill it.

Contents

Foreward

As Connecticut Visiting Nurses Association's Hospice Administrator, "expressive puppetry" was not high on my list of priorities when it was first called to my attention. I was concerned with meeting regulations, staffing issues, census growth, and building a clinically and financially sound program. And it may have remained below my radar screen for a while longer, had it not been for the fact that I was working on a budget and noticed it was an expense item. I was about to delete it from my spreadsheet when I remembered the interview for the position I held. I was asked if I would integrate services such as expressive arts, expressive puppetry, and massage therapy into the services Connecticut VNA provided for patients and their families. I gave what seemed to be a reasonable and accommodating answer: "Yes, I most certainly will."

Had it not been for that answer, I might have made a regrettable mistake and deleted expressive puppetry – and Marge Schneider– from my budget and from my professional life.

Marge had worked for several years in expressive puppetry and she spoke of doing this kind of work as a privilege and honor. I decided one day to observe her at work with our patients. Marge greeted the staff and inquired about the patient we were to see: a woman who suffered from dementia and qualified for hospice services. That meant she was bound to her bed and needed full assistance; she was losing weight and was unable to communicate meaningfully, limited to a vocabulary of a dozen words or less. I reviewed her chart before Marge and I entered her room. The chart was thick and heavy. The patient was eighty-three years old and had been living at the nursing facility for twelve years. When she first came to the facility she had adjusted remarkably well. She participated in most of the recreational events and had been a pleasant presence in the hallways and dining area, greeting other residents, visitors, and staff with a warm smile and friendly chatter. Over the past three years her health and deteriorated, so that there was little left of that cheerful, magnanimous woman.

Marge greeted the patient, but she gave no response – no vocal acknowledgment, no change in facial expression, no movement at all. She was the kind of patient that people tend to talk around, not to. She was the kind that most people, including myself, might instinctively relate to as an object rather than a person because there seems so little of the person there. Marge, however, continued talking with her as if unaware of her lack of response, as if the patient were just as much a person as Marge herself.

Marge understood that the first rule of caring is to treat a client with dementia as a person. We sometimes comfort ourselves with the thought that, as the disease progresses, the victim loses awareness of what he or she has lost and is losing. But there are many signs that some awareness is there; the anxiety, restlessness, and behavioral symptoms we identify and treat in these patients indicate that something definitely is going on. We medicate those symptoms because we often know no other way to mitigate them.

Marge sat on the patient's bed, brought her face close to her and began speaking. Marge asked her questions and sang to her as she opened her bag of puppets and brought them out one by one. Marge started out with a butterfly puppet, telling a story as the butterfly "flew" in graceful arcs, alighting now and then on her arm, her shoulder, then her cheek. The patient's face remained stony. Marge wasn't daunted by the patient's lack of enthusiasm and immediately began to double her own. I noticed an energy between the two women. In fact, it seemed to me that Marge was generating the energy of three or four people. Another puppet came out, this one a large purple bird. It danced as Marge sang. Still nothing. Marge's zeal didn't wane. She brought out the next puppet, a black Labrador retriever. The pup lapped at the patient's face and wagged its tail in expectation of a pat on the head or an encouraging word. It received neither, but neither did it show any sign of disappointment. A few more puppets made their appearances: a chipmunk, a robin, and a little girl.

Nothing.

Marge refused to quit. She continued singing, talking, and telling stories, her face inches away from the patient's. Finally, a little kitten puppet crawled from Marge's bag and made its gentle way up the patient's belly and chest and nestled on her neck, its face nuzzling the woman's cheek. It was astonishing: the muscles in her face relaxed and her features softened. She actually put her hand on the kitten's back. At this point, Marge told her a story about the kitten. The kitten, it seemed, loved to play and roll around on the floor and cuddle, but often the kitten would leave the house and wander around outside, meeting with other small animals. As Marge was explaining this to the patient, the woman interrupted her in a weak, unsteady voice: "But she always comes home."

The response took me a bit off guard for a couple of reasons. I was distracted by my own thoughts – thinking of what to say to Marge after what I thought would be a valiant but failed effort to reach this woman. Second, the last thing I expected from this patient was anything resembling a whole sentence. I had read her chart and knew our criteria for hospice certification: she was not able to fashion sentences. The most I expected were utterances of single words. But she had formed a complete sentence and there she was, petting the kitten puppet as a tear rolled down her cheek. Marge let the kitten stay with her for a while and promised they would come back to see her soon. The patient smiled and said, "Bye."

I left the room feeling I had witnessed something important, perhaps, in a small way, miraculous. Not miraculous in the traditional sense of the word – not a cure or a recovery – but miraculous in a palliative sense. Here was a person who lived her life in isolation, unable to connect to anything outside herself. But in those few moments with Marge she had connected to something: a kitten. For a brief while, she was a child again, delighting in the kitten's affection, delighting in the thought that this creature loved her, delighting in what we all delight in: giving and receiving affection.

Marge's interaction with the patient did something for me that all my previous experience with severely demented individuals had not done. It humanized and demystified the person inside the dementia. It had often seemed to me that people who suffered from Alzheimer's and other dementias became something other than themselves, something unlike their real selves.

Marge visited this patient many more times, and each time the woman took pleasure in her kitten because, as she said that first session, it always came home.

The interaction between Marge and the patient made me think of my grandmother who had suffered from dementia. During her last years, there was something ghostly about her (my son, only three at the time, could see it, too). Her cold hands reached out for a comfort she would no longer be able to receive. It was as if she was there enough to know she was not there. She was a lost soul who couldn't accept that she had died and lingered in a world with which she could no longer interact, suspended between being and non-being and not knowing how to get to either.

What if someone like Marge had come to our home and spent some time and attention with my grandmother, finding the person hidden by dementia? What might those months have been like if my grandmother had been engaged by someone like Marge? What if someone had found that something, that kitten, with which she could engage and interact? What if my son, instead of only hearing her confused and desperate cries for help, had been able to connect with his great-grandmother, play with her and the puppet, and see her as something other than scary and strange?

That would have made all the difference for my family. And that's the difference Marge and her expressive puppetry brought to the patients and families of our hospice program.

When a gift is given, such as the one Marge brought to our patients, people notice. Patients and families notice, other health care professionals notice. We may not erect billboards telling the world about our hospice's expressive puppetry program, but the word gets out. Our hospice program operates in five locations in Connecticut and we noticed that referrals increased in those locations we offered puppetry. Needless to say, we have expanded the expressive puppetry program to cover all our locations. We have found that a commitment to excellence and meaningful care to patients and their families can take the shape of a butterfly or a dog or a kitten that always returns home.

Tim Boone, Former Vice President
Hospice and Palliative Care of CT VNA

Acknowledgments

Wow! I can't believe that my manuscript is finally a completed publication and I am so grateful that it made its way into your hands. Never imagining that it would take more than ten years to complete, I owe a debt of gratitude to a host of family members, friends, and colleagues who gave valuable feedback on its content and style. This book became a family project. My heart is so full of love and gratitude for my husband David and our two sons, Seth and Jared, who are a continual precious and loving presence in our lives. David never wavered in his unending love and support, always readily available to lend a discerning ear or offer an invaluable comment or suggestion. He remains my continual source of humor, optimism and patience, always holding the faith when mine begins to waver. Seth so generously and lovingly took on the final laborious editing project with sensitivity, unending patience, meticulous skill and great insight to help make the manuscript clearer and more readable. He gently and lovingly but firmly encouraged me to delete certain stories that he saw as redundant but for me were so treasured and precious in my memory that it was too difficult for me to do alone. He then with open heart took on the challenge of photographing my puppets in the professional photography studio of our friends Pat and Ed Deguzis of Deguzis Photography in Hartford, Connecticut who so generously gifted us their space. Jared's well-thought out and creative final review and modifications of the artistic layout and text was a result of numerous hours at the computer, first diligently and skillfully learning the necessary program and then spending much time enhancing the photographs which proved invaluable to the overall aesthetic quality of this book. Along with his fiancée, Crystal Byler, they used their creative talents and skills to develop the design and layout for the cover. A loving thank you to you Crystal. Vince Whitman, a long-time friend, took the title of this book seriously and actually lent his hand, well two of them to be precise, and patiently sat for hours while Jared and Crystal painted away. A big thank you to you too Vince.

My brother, Jack Durell, MD, a psychiatrist, provided thoughtful comments and suggestions which enhanced the book's quality. Deep gratitude goes to John Surowiecki and Jane Rufus Blanshard for lending their professional editing skills so openheartedly and generously in their initial readings. Blessings to Sigh Buchannan, colleague; Nancy Pearce, friend and colleague and author of *Inside Alzheimer's*, an important book in the field; and Eileen Atherton, an insightful and brilliant therapist and treasured friend who read the book several times and lovingly helped to move me forward with great insight and skill. Our friend, Abba Caspi, during a brainstorming session together, helped to discover the title and kept me on track as my computer guru. Our daughter-in-law, Rina, was always ready and willing to offer her expertise regarding questions of design which was most appreciated and valued. A special thank you goes to my graphic designer, Kristen Wartschow of Burlington, Connecticut. She remained calm and patient, always open and consistently flexible, willing to offer more options until one resonated with me. I enjoyed working with her.

I embrace the memory of Nancy Cole who died in July 1996, after a long and valiant struggle with cancer. Nancy lived in Canada and was the puppet therapy consultant for Puppeteers of America. She was a nurse, professional puppeteer and puppetry instructor for students of all ages, a creative arts therapist, and author of "Lend Them a Hand – Therapeutic Puppetry". I was deeply impressed and moved by her vibrant and positive spirit, her deep sense of humanity, and her creativity, love, warmth, and passion. She cheered me on as I lay inroads for my work with puppets and adults. Even when ill, she remained supportive, anxious to talk with me on the phone since she no longer could travel to conferences in the

U.S. Nancy's life embodied the aspiration of her quote, which I take to heart, "We are not simply God's puppets, we can be God's puppeteers." Her spirit continues to cheer me on.

I wish to thank the Falk Foundation for Excellence for awarding me a grant over a decade ago to write this book and I am grateful for their confidence and support of my work. A special thanks goes to Carrie Falk, the inspiration behind the foundation and one of the most dynamic, creative, and effervescent people I know.

Finally and most importantly, I owe a debt of gratitude to the people with whom I worked for over twenty years in long-term care and hospice. They are the major contributors to this undertaking. It has been a process of listening, learning and recording. They have been some of my finest teachers and greatest inspirations. They remain in my heart as I share their wisdom, courage and love with the world.

Heartfelt gratitude to all of the activity professionals, child and adolescent psychiatrists, marriage and family therapists, social workers, and other professionals in the healing arts with whom I connected during the past twenty years and who have so generously provided their stories and urged me to share what I have learned from my work. Unfortunately, throughout the decade, I have lost touch with many of these kind, skilled and wonderful people but have made every effort to provide credit and offer my sincere apologies for any inadvertent omissions. I am uncertain if they still hold their title or reside in the same location.

This book is based largely on the experiences of these sensitive, creative, and inspiring people. We stimulated, motivated, and nurtured each other. To all of you, I am deeply indebted and grateful. It is your thirst to explore this arena, your vision, and your generosity in sharing your stories that have helped to make this book what it is.

Introduction

Only serendipity accounts for the path that led me to expressive puppetry. I began my career as a pre-kindergarten and elementary school teacher, and then spent the next nine years raising my children. After that, I decided to find a creative outlet that would supplement our family finances. As Valentine's Day approached in 1985, my thoughts turned to chocolate, one of my passions, and I began designing an array of chocolate delicacies. One of the early venues I sold my wares at was a teddy bear show and I came with enough chocolate bears to fill a six-foot table. Inspired by the throngs of attendees' joyful reaction to the merchandise – plush bears of every size, clothing and furniture for bears, bear quilts, and now edible chocolate teddy bears – I joined the teddy bear circuit as a vendor. I had great fun creating unique designs, but under the guise of quality control I (deliciously!) consumed my way to hypoglycemia and had to abandon my chocolate bears.

I wanted to develop a product line that did not rely on chocolate. My husband David and I decided to attend a trade show in New York City. Its vastness, as we walked each aisle, thoroughly exhausted us. We took a reprieve by entering a magical and whimsical booth filled with an extensive variety of puppets. Our laughter as we began to play with the puppets seemed to lessen our fatigue. I gravitated to a charming turtle puppet, intrigued by how it could withdraw into its shell. I was captivated by its potential to lure a shy child out of her own shell, and perhaps coax out a word or smile. We took this little critter home with us, unaware of the effect it would have on the adult clients I would later come to work with. Accompanying the turtle were several large, highly expressive bear puppets with different color fur and intriguing personalities that would soon make their way into the homes and hearts of the enthusiasts in our teddy bear world.

While attending a teddy bear festival, I was approached by an activity director from a nursing home who was intrigued by the connective power of one of our bear puppets. She thought a puppet like ours could have a positive effect on nursing home residents.

We were invited to an activity professional's workshop and were warmly and enthusiastically received. Through word of mouth, invitations to attend other conferences began coming our way, and we expanded our collection of puppets. We were heartened by the many accounts of nursing home residents whose spirits were lifted by the puppets and who, silent for years, had begun to connect with and respond to the world outside. Small miracles were taking place every day. The enthusiasm of the professionals we met was infectious and inspiring.

David and I began traveling throughout the country appearing at nearly forty conferences a year, mostly therapeutically-oriented events for attendees such as child and adolescent psychiatrists, marriage and family therapists, and social workers. As they visited our booth, I showed them the ways that the puppets could be used, demonstrating techniques and intuitively addressing specific client issues. As they provided additional information about their patients, I would help them select appropriate puppets. Our colorful, unique, and lovable critters not only lured the attendees into our magical space, but helped to stimulate an environment for a creative exchange of ideas and inspirational approaches for client interactions.

It was at one of these conferences that I vividly recall meeting a short, stocky man with a generous smile who joyfully interacted with the numerous critters on display and enthusiastically supported my work with the puppets. I later learned that this intriguing man was Jim Brennan, an author, health-care trainer, and consultant who used puppets to teach, inspire, and touch many people's lives. He became a guiding and motivational force in my professional life.

At the same time, David and I began to present a variety of themed, age-appropriate, therapeutic, and spiritually-based programs at skilled-nursing homes, assisted-living centers, and adult-day-care facilities in several states – all incorporating puppets, storytelling, and music. Captivated by the therapeutic healing power of puppets, we began to dramatically increase the number of puppets that we offered for adoption. In 1989, thanks to the creativity and effort of David, our son, Jared, and our late friend, Gail Morris, we transformed our barn into what Jared named "The Puppet Petting Zoo". Our Zoo became home to one of the largest collections of puppets in the country and was housed in a variety of "natural habitats." Individuals and groups used our facility as a resource center for hands-on educational play, storytelling, and puppet therapy and were able to adopt the puppets for their personal and professional use.

Around that time, I began to enhance my clinical skills through training in spiritual counseling from Alice Raim, a skillful and compassionate social worker, and from Rabbi Steven Steinberg, a highly-knowledgeable clergyman, under a special program created by the New Haven Jewish Family Service. I also pursued training in other therapeutic modalities, became a Reiki practitioner, and took classes in meditation, visualization, and yoga.

Much of my motivation for working with people suffering from dementia and depression came from my experiences with my own parents. My father, whom I dearly loved, lived with us for the final three years of his life when he had severe dementia. Living with him increased my understanding of how this disease worked and motivated me to find insight into his veiled world. In addition, my mother lived in our house for the last eight years of her life. Her struggles with depression were exacerbated by a stroke she suffered late in life. Trying to enhance her quality of life during those final years led me to develop ways of communicating with her as well.

In 2001, I had the opportunity to begin working with a highly-skilled and compassionate hospice team at Hospice and Palliative Care of Connecticut. Paul Truby, Director of Counseling Services, was able to see beyond the stereotype that puppets were only for children and had faith that puppets can tap into the child within us all. Together, we pioneered a program that used puppets,music, storytelling, Reiki, meditation, visualization, and poetry. For fifteen years, I had worked with people with dementia in group settings and so I was grateful for the opportunity to work one-on-one with clients and their families for five fulfilling and rewarding years. It was indeed a privilege and honor when they admitted me into their private, sacred space and I was able to add a moment of joy, peace, comfort, and understanding. I was grateful for the opportunity to enrich a client's final days and thankful for all that my clients taught me. I have experienced a full range of emotions in being privy to their fears and joys, loneliness and despair, hopes and dreams, courage, healing and, in most cases, their journey to the next place.

Through a Pedi-Pal program in support of hospice pediatric-care, I was able to use my early childhood and elementary education teaching experience along with expressive puppetry, music, and storytelling techniques. Chronically ill, these children came to us with a significant expectation for recovery. I worked with them, as well as their siblings and parents, attempting to bring play and laughter, understanding and acceptance, communication and emotional release, and love and hope into their lives.

I am now involved in presenting short hands-on, interactive workshops and trainings called "A Hand in Healing: Compassionate Caring Connections". These provide innovative techniques and insights that can be quickly and easily learned and used to dramatically impact people who are often uncooperative and non-communicative. I was frequently asked by health-care professionals to write a book explaining how I have used puppets to reach people who were thought of as unreachable. These professionals understood the value of puppetry in health care but needed some guidance on how to move forward with this modality. Others were already working with puppets when we met and generously shared their inspiring stories and creative ideas, but still wanted new ways to further their practice and deepen the connections with their clients. This book is for all of them – in sincere appreciation of their openness to new ideas and respect for their vision and courage.

In writing this book, I honor all my clients, the brave and inspirational people who will remain forever in my heart. Many of these wonderful people, because of dementia or depression, were often seen by family members and professional caregivers as no longer being able to share anything worthwhile. Too many times, these individuals were not offered an opportunity to tell their story. They remained silent, their spirit often broken and stifled. This book, I hope, does its small part to end that silence.

I have chosen to work with puppets as a mostly non-verbal way to connect. It is my way to invite that person's expression of life that is often hidden inside to come forth and meet the light within me. However, the essence is not, I believe, in the level of skill and expertise in the art of puppetry but rather in the depth, authenticity, and intent of the connection. A puppet has the potential to bring wonder, love, and playfulness into the life of any person with whom you interact. I am excited by what you will soon discover as you bring a puppet to life. Who knows where your imagination will take you, what experiences you will be privileged to share, the love you will kindle as you begin to explore a powerful tool, a magical ally – a puppet! However, whether you bring to life a puppet or use other tools in your practice, I encourage you to look inside yourself for your own strengths and unique talents and discover how this book will enrich and deepen your healing connections with the people with whom you interact.

Chapter 1

Opening Hearts, Creating Connection

The Power of Puppet Therapy

Let us knock gently at each other's heart, glad for a chance to look within.

–Carole Haynes

A Barometer For Daniel's Emotional Healing

"What's that sleazebag doing here?" growled Daniel, as the bear puppet sniffed at his cheek. This was Daniel's first expression of anger and rejection since I had begun visiting him several weeks earlier. In fact, Daniel had consistently closed himself to any display of emotion or bonding with me or my puppets. His simple, bitter outburst was a quick and fleeting glimpse into a depth of emotion that had been well masked until this moment. I was grateful for this unveiling, albeit brief window, to his authentic voice. However, he refused to explore his emotions. His constant indifference and rejection triggered an intuitive response on my part and I told him that I was going to shorten my visit on this particular day but I would return next week. "The 'sleazebag' puppet and I feel unwelcome." Daniel pulled his head back slightly, as if surprised by my response, and then a look of dismay came over his face; but he did not attempt to stop me from leaving. All he said was a dutiful 'goodbye.'

Totally paralyzed, Daniel, a man in his early fifties with multiple sclerosis, was confined to a nursing-home bed. His ruddy face, swollen from his medications, was incongruous with his otherwise handsome, well-defined features. Apathy was his major defense at this time in his life. He insisted that nothing mattered to him and kept his emotions tightly guarded. He seemed to have given up. He rarely spoke and offered little insight into what was going on inside. His biggest sense of relief seemed to come from a retreat into sleep and that is all he wanted to do.

Still, I was convinced that a part of him remained attentive during my visits. He was sleeping less and his eyes were often alert as he focused on each puppet and seemed to listen to the music, the meditations, the readings, and the poems, although he still rarely responded. During my weekly visits, I worked relentlessly to open him to the life around and within him, but with little success. Frequent visits from his siblings and other loving family members did not help to spark a connection.

However, upon returning the next week, Daniel smiled as I entered his room, a smile that appeared genuine and heartfelt and provided me with a sense of warmth and hope. This display of welcoming and mild affection was atypical and took me by surprise. He actually said he was happy to see me which was a major step. As the weeks went on, he began to open to his story as he gained trust and confidence in me. However, whenever he shared his anger, it was always accompanied by a self-deprecating smile, as if what he was feeling was really not that important. He seemed always to consider himself to be the one at fault and unworthy of any understanding or love. Eventually, his story began to fully unfold. He spoke of a wife who had betrayed him. She had taken another man into her life, parading this handsome, physically able new lover in front of her disabled husband. It was only as Daniel began to acknowledge his pain and share his grief and anger that he could open himself to deeper, more intimate connections, whether from me or his extended family.

I eventually learned a small but important piece of information for my work: as a farmer for most of his life, Daniel had once dearly loved his border collie. Over a period of several weeks, I introduced him to my border collie puppet and many of my other farm animal puppets, which became the catalysts for his stories. The border collie served as a barometer for Daniel's emotions. When he was in a good mood, he smiled and allowed a connection to unfold that was at times intimate and joyful, gently petting the puppet, allowing it to nuzzle his neck and offer other forms of affection. When he was in a dark place he projected that negativity onto those around him, closing off to me and pushing away the puppets.

After many months, Daniel began to express the sadness and anger he was feeling about his life. He no longer responded with, "I don't care," and his depression slowly began to lift. He became brighter and more hopeful and experienced a resurgent sense of humor and renewed caring about his life and the people who genuinely were concerned about him and loved him. He discovered in himself an unexpected courage to confront his feelings, his limitations, and his vulnerabilities. With this courage, he was able to release the anger, the blame, the sense of injustice, and even the pain itself. As he began to heal and find some inner peace, the border collie puppet was not always needed. On his own, Daniel was able to reclaim the peace he so deeply wanted before he closed his circle of life.

Miracles Are Everywhere

The effects of depression and cognitive impairment, such as dementia, ripple out beyond the person who is suffering from the condition. When someone's heart is in retreat or their cognitive abilities are impaired, it can have a profound effect on those of us who love or care for them. If we are a caregiver or service provider, we may at times feel helpless in our ability to connect with our client. If this is a loved one, it might seem as if the person has become a vacant shell who cannot be reached. This can be a deeply discouraging and difficult position. I felt compelled to write this book to share my experiences and those of numerous healthcare professionals to offer a ray of light. My approach may be untraditional, but it has proven effective in breaking down the barriers of dementia and depression and providing an alternative approach that provides hope, inspiration, and understanding.

I have found that puppets can sometimes seem to be magical in their ability to connect hearts, minds, and spirits—and to provide moments of joy. Something from deep within emerges, and a profound, sometimes startling link can take place. Whether used in hospitals, nursing homes, mental health facilities, or bereavement support services, puppets positively affect the people on both sides of the interaction. A puppet can break the ice and lead the way to establishing a trusting, nonthreatening relationship. A puppet can help a client, patient, or loved one connect to a genuine sense of self, promoting spontaneity, openness, and honesty. A puppet can provide a creative outlet, helping patients express their pain and struggles, make sense of their situation, and come to some resolution about a problem in a creative, relaxed, and loving manner. Puppets can be a dynamic therapeutic tool whether used alone or in combination with other techniques.

Over the years, I have heard from many professionals who have worked successfully with puppets. Their stories have inspired and encouraged me in my work. I have heard about nursing-home residents who had not communicated in years beginning to talk. Clients who had been unreachable will start to open up and share their stories. Patients are calmed enough to undergo frightening surgical procedures. The stories I've heard, and my firsthand experiences, have shown me that puppets help to unlock feelings, assimilate traumas, lift spirits, and reestablish a sense of connectedness.

These miracles, large and small, are everywhere. For example:

- In a health-care facility in Memphis, Tennessee, a simple little puppet, called Muley, brings together a group of elderly residents through writing plays and sharing stories and intergenerational experiences.

- In a bereavement-counseling group in Everett, Washington, two camel puppets, named Hope and Pride, help adults tell their stories and share how they feel about the loss of their loved ones.

- In an acute-care facility in New Haven, Connecticut, a frog puppet entices a hospitalized eighteen-year-old girl to explore issues that her child-life specialist alone could not uncover.

- In a pastoral-care and counseling center in Abilene, Texas, a therapist, with the aid of a sheep puppet, helps a twenty-one-year-old selective mute to talk.

- In a hospital in Washington, DC, an elderly woman is calmed for surgery through the use of a doctor puppet.

- In a child and adolescent psychiatrist's office in New Jersey, a three and one-half year old girl is able to share her traumatic story of sexual abuse only after the psychiatrist incorporates the child's rabbit puppet into the therapeutic sessions.

Throughout my twenty years of working with puppets, I've witnessed that whenever a person and puppet connect – no matter how tense the individual might be—his or her body language and facial expression will

typically soften when interaction with a puppet begins. The puppet elicits a twinkle in the eye, a touch, a laugh, a hug, or even a conversation. A connection is made with the individual's inner child, which often promotes authentic sharing of one's stories.

A puppet can assist you in getting to know your client and determine where he or she is in the healing process. As with Daniel, the puppet can act as an emotional barometer. When Daniel was unwilling to express his emotions or was angry, he would ignore the puppet or else express anger and disgust with it. When he was in a better mood, he was able to interact with the border collie puppet in an affectionate, loving way.

Enabling Communication

Everyone has a story to tell. A puppet can be a catalyst in enabling the person to share what lies deep within. The puppet can serve as a conduit for pent-up emotions, allowing for cathartic release. When a person animates a puppet, it can become an extension of his inner world, allowing him to express his feelings, ultimately leading to acceptance, comfort, and healing. When you animate a puppet, it can serve as an intermediary, allowing you to speak indirectly to patients, letting them know that it's all right to express whatever they are thinking and feeling without shame, guilt, or fear.

A twenty-one year old select mute had been seeking counsel from a pastoral counselor but for weeks on end, the patient controlled the world around him through his silence. The counselor could not motivate any verbal interchange and was at a loss of how to proceed. Out of sheer frustration, he picked up a sheep puppet that was lying about in his office and with no clear insight in how to proceed, simply picked it up, put his hand in its mouth and vocalized a spirited "baa". The silence was immediately broken as the patient echoed his own "baa". The counselor then resounded with a "baa baa" and that was immediately reciprocated with a "baa baa". This interchange of voices went on for forty-five minutes until the patient responded with a "baa baa baa baa baa baa THIRSTY!!!" The counselor immediately secured a drink for his client and it was as if a dam had broken. Upon having his request met, the young man burst forth in an unstoppable rampage that continued into each and every session until the healing process began to take hold.

Traditional verbal approaches can fall short when clients and patients are too scared or reluctant to discuss their traumas, have aphasia, or lack the cognitive skills to clearly express themselves verbally. But their voices can be recovered. When a client is able to open to a puppet, he can open to a depth and range of authentic emotion. Recognition of those feelings can then be identified. The puppet can serve as a bridge to the client, providing useful information for you and inner peace for him or her.

Matthew: Moving Beyond Confusion and Depression

Matthew was in his seventies and dying of cancer. A tall, slim man with dark, intense eyes, Matthew had severe dementia. From the beginning, he was open and receptive to my visits, readily engaged by the puppets, and profoundly touched by the sound of the Native American flute I played for him. He immediately reached out to hold and pet the golden retriever puppet and, as weeks went by, their bond became closer. At times I felt like a voyeur, privy to so intimate and meaningful a relationship.

Matthew was gentle and endearing. He often wept as he interacted with the golden retriever puppet and despite his limited verbal ability, I began to gain some insight into his past and into the profound grief and regret he was trying to express. As he hugged the puppet, he focused on areas of his life that were clearly upsetting but difficult for him to fully articulate. He uttered phrases, "separate beds" was one that he repeated often and which seemed to hold significant meaning for him. Intuitively, I began to assume that perhaps Matthew was experiencing a deep regret over a lack of connection and love with his wife.

Eventually, in order to find appropriate ways to empathize and effectively define and respond to his truth about his world, I made an appointment to meet his wife. Without breaching confidentiality, I asked many open-ended questions and began to receive an outpouring of heartfelt replies. Her relationship with Matthew had been estranged, and she felt that, in a sense, she had lived a lie. They had indeed slept in separate beds and were emotionally detached. She had never wanted their children or extended family to know the depth of their unhappiness and incompatibility and so she had always put up a good front. Sharing her truth was freeing; the experience was so positive and rewarding for her that she enthusiastically welcomed the return visit from our team's very skilled

social worker, Barbara Girard, to further assist her in coming to some acceptance, forgiveness, and peace.

In the meantime, Matthew was increasingly becoming attached to my eagle puppet which offered a way for him to express and explore his fears of death and dying. I talked about the potential for beauty and peace as one gets ready to close one's circle of life. Matthew consistently expressed the good he wanted to do in the "next place." "I want to go home, he cried, as soon as possible. I am getting old and my heart is getting weaker." Although this was difficult for us to fully explore, these conversations seemed to allow him to forgive himself for his shortcomings and limitations in his physical time on earth. Listening to the flute helped him to become increasingly calm and, after many months, his weeping stopped and his fears, guilt, and anxieties seemed to vanish. At this point, he no longer needed me or my puppets but he remained consistently open and welcoming to his wife's visits. Fortunately for himself and for those who loved him, he was able to close his circle of life with an inner peace.

Puppets For All Ages

Therapists often tell me that they recognize the value of puppets and would use them…if they only worked with children. This is an unfortunate misconception. Puppets are not only for children. People of all ages can identify with puppets. Often, a person will readily bond and communicate with a puppet because it offers unconditional love, is nonthreatening and non-judgmental, and asks nothing in return. Of course, if you are uncomfortable working with puppets, then they will not be a useful aid to your practice, no matter what the age of the patient. But if you are open to the playfulness and spontaneity that puppets often bring forth in people, then many of your clients, young and old, can benefit. True, there can be resistance, but there is a part of each of us that wants to respond to playfulness and spontaneity. If a therapist is willing to take a risk, persevere, and run with his or her creativity and imagination, barriers can dissolve.

Barry Sultanoff, a deeply sensitive and passionate physician, has eagerly and joyously adopted puppets for use in his treatment methodologies. As Barry says, "Professional life here becomes animated and full of surprise awakenings. There need be no artificial separation between what is 'mature adult' and what is 'healthy child.' Unpredictability is a friend and spontaneity a welcome healer!"

Chapter 2

Love Heals

Making a Soulful Connection

There is a voice that doesn't use words.

Listen.

-Rumi

I believe that each patient I work with has within, just like me, a need to be valued and respected, a need to connect, a need to speak and to be heard, and a right to be emotionally and spiritually alive. How a person may appear externally often gives no hint of his true essence nor is it a window into his soul. I earnestly believe that it is essential that people not be categorized and put into boxes. The risk and danger of prejudgment is a loss of potential connection to the beauty in another. To assume and treat an individual as a vacant shell that does not need connection and interaction will have significant impact on that person's emotional and spiritual survival and well-being.

Our time, our very presence, is the greatest gift we can give to another person. Sometimes we draw on our own life experiences and sometimes on the deepest instincts of our hearts. We, the health-care providers and caregivers, are not the focus. It is not about the telling of our story or about our talents, our ability to articulate, our education or our knowledge. It's not even about our technical skills as musicians, artists, or puppeteers. It is about using our insights, talents, skills, knowledge, and sensitivity – to make a connection with the soul of another person. Everyone has a story to share, our challenge is to be able to successfully encourage their telling and then to be able to fully listen in whatever form it is presented, with our eyes, ears, heart, and undivided attention.

As the physician and poet Oliver Wendell Holmes wrote, "Alas for those that never sing, but die with all their music in them!" And so I strive to help individuals recognize their song, get in tune with themselves, and sing it out before they close their circle of life.

How to Connect Soulfully with a Patient

Whether you call it spirituality, intention, soulfulness, or use a different term, I have found the greatest success when I use a spiritual approach to my interactions with patients. I will share with you what I am aware of within me when I work with a patient. My challenge is to help you envision a process that goes beyond words by attempting to take you with me into my world.

In the beginning of my day, I take a moment for a prayer of intention. I ask for help from the universe to be unconditionally present, meet my client where he or she is and offer help and healing. I empty myself of judgments, expectations, and biases so that I can open myself to the godliness and beauty within each soul. My job is to listen – to really listen – to be aware of all internal and external cues. I allow love to be my teacher and intuition my guide. I attempt to create a safe and sacred space based on mutual respect with the hope that we can explore self and spirit and allow experiences to unfold in a direction of truth, authenticity, and deeper meaning.

When we really listen and genuinely care, we may be able to help others move beyond their limitations, isolation, and loneliness. That's why it is vital that we are fully present, and not distracted or divided in our attention. Our body language needs to be relaxed and open to increase opportunities for connection. I typically sit up close, leaning forward and looking directly into my client's eyes.

I take several deep, heartfelt breaths before I enter my client's room. No matter what I may be experiencing in my life, no matter what worries, stresses, or concerns I may have, once I arrive at a client's bedside I allow myself to be fully present with no agenda. Through meditation, music, yoga, and dance I have learned to empty my mind and put aside the "I" in order to focus on the "you." I allow the clients to guide the way, and I am led intuitively by their needs and wants. I let go of my need to know or be right. I attempt to interact without fears, insecurities, or preconceived notions and find some aspect of the client that I can find worthy and genuinely admire so that a quality connection can be established. This is especially important when working with patients with a criminal background or a history of being abusive.

I always ask permission when I enter a person's sacred space, wanting to ascertain that the timing is right and that they are willing to open to my presence. I also always make certain that they want to meet my puppet and that they are willing to open to the puppet's touch and interaction. If I genuinely listen and observe, the potential to express his preference is always present. If he agrees, I first hold my puppet up within his visual range and then use my observational skills to note his level of comfort or stress. I watch his eyes, body language, and rate of breathing to assess his level of comfort if words are not forthcoming.

Tips for Working with Dementia Patients

With persons with dementia, the initial connection is established through the eyes. Before opening up, the client peers intently into my eyes as if searching my soul and penetrating deep within my being. My sense is that they are searching for a comfort level, a sense of security. It appears they are waiting for an invitation to step out and be accepted for who they are without judgment. They cannot typically verbally process and interrogate, so they question and probe intuitively – silently. I talk to them as if the potential for understanding is always present. After a time, their eyes come to a level of rest, acceptance, and comfort, and they become ready to open and connect. It is as if I must pass a test for entrance into their private lives. The sharing of an initial heartfelt smile seems to signal the emergence and the awakening of a connection. This is the beginning of trust.

After looking into each other's eyes we begin to gently look into each other's hearts, not seeking an answer but attempting to listen to the song within. There is not a moment where we attempt to fix or change each other. It is as if we both understand that we are unique and sacred, perfectly imperfect just as we are. Our connection is based solely on natural honoring, compassion, and unconditional love. When our voice is heard and our spirit is honored, we are more apt to have the courage to take on life. We both learn to relax into the comfort, security, and beauty of appreciating and validating each other for who we are – no masks, no camouflage, no ulterior motives.

You will now meet and hopefully be inspired by a few of the people with whom I have been privileged to work. These people chose to open their hearts and permit me to enter the sacred realm of their soul. Their stories are unchanged and pure, only their names are different. It is a challenge for me however to put into words the profound magnitude of intimacy that often connected us. How the puppets helped me reach beyond the barriers of dementia and depression is their magic.

Emma: A Spiritual Awakening

Emma, a woman in her eighties with white hair, a ruddy complexion, and advanced dementia, rarely spoke and seemed to be in her own world. When I first met Emma I asked her if I could spend some time with her, as I ask of all my clients. She responded clearly, with a look of disbelief.

"You ask me if you can stay? It's your place."

"Oh, no," I replied, "It's your home, and I am merely your guest."

Tears welled up as Emma continued to stare deeply into my eyes. Her spirit seemed to lift as her eyes brightened. She looked around her room, as if for the first time, and commented, "It's really pretty here. You're so sweet." Emma proceeded to compliment my clothes, hair, and even my teeth. Her world took on a beauty for her, and she chose, on that day, to allow me into her world as a friend and confidante.

When I began to animate various puppets, Emma seemed uncomfortable and said that they were for children, but I assured her that they are for the child within us all. She seemed to accept this premise and open to the joy they provided. She seemed to most readily bond with the sheepdog puppet. They looked like they belonged together, with their snow-white hair, both seeming vulnerable and huggable. She seemed mesmerized as I animated the puppet, smiling as it showered her with affection. Emma continued to open to the love and magic around her and remained in a place of engagement, responsiveness, and connectedness to include both me and the puppet she chose to embrace. As Emma opened to this nurturing connection, she remembered a story of when she was a child and one of her animals died.

There were certain puppets that helped to open Emma's spirit and only then would she be amazingly clear and articulate. At these times, she was able to put appropriate words together and communicate thoughts and feelings that had been severely compromised for years. The butterfly puppet helped move Emma into a more spiritual realm and she would allude to heaven, death, and dying. "Time is getting short," she clearly said on one of our visits.

One spring morning, Emma seemed quiet and introspective. "Are you feeling sad?" I asked.

"Very! I feel all mixed up," Emma quietly responded. She began crying, saying that she was very tired. "I want to go home," she said. "And sometimes I don't. I want to get out of here. I don't want them to see how happy I am to get out of here. An hour ago, I was ready to go."

I asked how I could best help, and she replied, "You can't. It's a short ride when ready." I assured Emma that she would close her cycle of life at just the right time and that one day we would meet again.

"Don't pass me by," she said tenderly. Staring deeply into my eyes with a newfound depth of connection, she added, "I always knew I knew you but now I am sure; I will stop whatever I am doing when we meet again."

I gently stroked Emma's arm, deeply touched by her willingness and courage to be real and honest − to open to a deeper level of intimacy in sharing her vulnerability and desire, her dreams and hopes and her warmth and depth of tender connection. Perhaps Emma was moved by the fact that there was someone who shared in deep connection with her and that in this moment, she no longer felt alone. What is precious is that a very real and beautiful connection occurred. We shared a soft, intimate cry together. "Why is my face getting wet?" Emma questioned, and, then, as though crying was unacceptable, she continued wistfully, "I always have to laugh."

"You don't have to now. It's okay to cry." I assured her. "I love you just the way you are and the way you are feeling is just perfect for right now." Emma seemed genuinely touched, her affect softened, and she seemed to radiate in the comfort of love and acceptance.

Whenever I brought the robin puppet to life, Emma opened to a sublime feeling of bliss. "I would like to go out with him. Wouldn't it be wonderful if one day I could fly with him? We'll go together." Emma had a vision of "the next place" that seemed to fill her with ecstasy. She was able to maintain that feeling of loving acceptance to all whom she looked at. For that moment in time, her world became bright with a powerful sense of hope and faith. Looking directly and serenely at me, she stated, "I can't describe you and all the beautiful things that light you up." In time, however, the sight of her small, drab, cheerless room clouded the beauty and she reflected, "Why can't there be some beauty right now, right here?" She experienced something that was real and honest. I could only fully listen and affirm the injustice of what she saw and felt and reassure her of my belief in the beauty of the "next place."

During another visit, I brought to life the metamorphic caterpillar puppet and alluded to the beauty within each of us. I spoke of how we might lose our hearing, eyesight, memory, and mobility, but our internal beauty – our connection to our internal source of love and light – remains intact. Emma's eyes began to well up, and she appeared deeply moved.

Toward the end of Emma's life, she did not always remember me as I approached her and initially seemed distant and cool. Her face, however, immediately brightened, and sometimes she was brought to tears by the beauty of the puppet I animated and her connection to it. After this interaction she would notice me again and with a surprised joyful look of recognition seemed delighted and grateful for my return.

On one particular day, however, Emma seemed belligerent and angry. Her every response was, "I don't care." I asked her what she did care about and she immediately and clearly responded, "I want to go home. I'm so tired; don't go away. I'm afraid of being without you." I assured her that her time would come and that she would close her circle of life at just the right time. "That's so kind of you." Her affect softened and she began to envision the loving, happy faces of her mother and sisters. "I'm ready. Oh, please! My mother is waiting. I see her in your smile. Please hurry. I want you to go with me." I suggested that I was not ready to close my circle of life but that one day we would meet again. "It will be a while, but I will be waiting for you." Emma said. She beamed as I played the Native American flute and then brought to life my butterfly puppet. She continued to smile as I read to her from the book "The Next Place". "That's what I want," Emma responded as I finished the reading. "Let's say good-bye. You better go. I can't stand you leaving. I want always to remember you. I love you."

I reassured her that I would always be in her heart and she in mine. "Fly back and get me; I'll wait for you. You're so good to me. I love you." She returned my love with the extraordinary gift of her own love which connects us together forever. Her blessings are still washing over me.

Belle and Roy: Mother and Son

Roy, a man in his thirties, was mentally challenged and lived at home with his parents. When awake, his mother Belle was alert, perky, and full of smiles and love. However, she was imminently dying and slept most of the time. As she had been his major caregiver and link to the outside world of activities and connection, Roy felt alone, fearful, and isolated.

Roy seemed open and receptive to my initial visit and readily engaged with the puppets. There was much laughter and amazement at how life-like the puppets were. Roy had once owned a dog, and we shared many stories about dogs. Together, we also sang a variety of cheerful, interactive songs. Over many weeks, he gradually began to relax and feel comfortable and safe with me. This allowed him to begin to express his feelings of fear and grief, and I was able to assure him of the naturalness of his experience. I encouraged him to let the tears flow. I believe that releasing his fear and sadness made space for joy and gratitude to emerge.

In time, Roy was able to talk about the many fun things he and his mother had experienced and could appreciate their happy times together. He was fearful that without his mother's presence he would not be able to retain his quality of life with its numerous connections and activities. With this revelation, I was able to realistically address his fears and put them to rest as there was already a very substantial, loving support system in place for him.

I helped Roy to understand and appreciate the normalcy of his feelings. I was then able to draw his attention to his notable strengths and abilities that were helping him cope in this difficult time. For the first time, the sadness in his eyes faded and they sparkled with a newfound faith and courage. He kept smiling with the thought of his newly realized strength. "I am strong, Mama!" he beamed.

Belle was delighted and comforted by his display of confidence. And Roy found solace in the thought that his mother would shine as the brightest star in the heavens and that her love would stay right with him in his heart. His courage enabled Belle to feel more secure in the fact that Roy would do well after her passing.

Frances: A Generous Spirit

As a child, Frances had been raised in foster homes after being removed from her abusive parents' home. However, many of her foster parents had also abused her. She could not remember ever being loved or treated with respect. As an adult, she had not established any loving, significant relationships and spent her time alone. Now in her sixties, Frances was confined to bed in a drab nursing home. A heavy woman, who was weak and jaundiced, she experienced physical and emotional pain. I was asked to visit her in an attempt to bring her some joyful connection. However, it was Frances who filled my heart with love and a sincere appreciation for her generosity of spirit.

Frances enjoyed the puppets that found their way into her arms, lighting up as they showered her with affection. She hugged each one tenderly, holding it close to her heart. No matter how much pain she was in she always rallied and welcomed the touch and loving connection of my puppets. Her weakened physical state never dampened her spirit; she always warmly smiled and joined me in song, taking my hand in hers. Despite the harsh realities of her life, she never seemed angry, bitter, or resentful. In fact, she was a gentle spirit who demonstrated patience and compassion, even for her roommate who was loud and invasive. Never did a friend or family member ever come to visit her but Frances always expressed appreciation for whatever it was that she did have in the moment.

She was always able to reach into her heart and find love and gratitude. I will long honor and treasure her memory and hold it deep in my heart.

Pauline: Sweet Serenity

Pauline, a woman with dementia, did not speak with words as we know them. Instead, her words were a succession of sounds that often came together in a melodic pattern. Confined to a hospital bed in her sister's home, she was the epitome of sweet serenity. There was a constant song in her heart evidenced by the gentle but constant movement of her head and beautiful smile.

Pauline's affect was rich with emotion. I was amazed by the clarity of our communication without her speaking a single recognizable word. Instead, her eyes and facial expressions clearly communicated her message. Pauline seemed equally adept at grasping the meaning behind the spoken word by resonating with its emotion. Pauline never seemed to get stuck in sadness and instead was able to identify and accept the feeling, shed some tears, and then let it go, making room for joy. She allowed her emotions to flow with grace and dignity. Pauline was quick to connect and express a depth of love and affection, readily reaching out to hold and embrace those fortunate enough to connect with her.

Pauline connected with puppets in the same way she did with people. She would reach out to the baby and butterfly puppets with tenderness and endearment. It seemed as if she appreciated the beauty of the butterfly, tenderly touching its wings. Her 'words' of endearment flowed as she interacted with the baby puppet. It was as if she was beaming with pride at its every movement. She also loved a monkey puppet that danced and a duck puppet that quacked, eliciting laughter and a rhythmic nodding of her head.

Pauline seemed to have a unique capacity to love fully and connect openly, without reservation. She was blessed with a soulfulness that transcended her inability to articulate words. She seemed to know the essence of meaningful connection and was able to engage in her life as fully as possible. Pauline is another treasure who will forever live within my heart.

Sharing the Vision

What an honor. What a privilege to connect with these profoundly unique and beautiful human beings. They came into my life, found a special place in my heart, and, truly, I shall never be the same. I believe that the reason we are here on this earth is to learn how to open to love, to connect and create endearing relationships and not to judge but to accept and honor the essence of the soul. Time changes the body but not always the heart. I feel both blessed and grateful to have had the privilege to look within the hearts of so many sacred souls. There is beauty within every living thing, and our challenge is to be able to identify, acknowledge, and honor that beauty. As we need and deserve to be loved and treasured for who we are, so, too, do we need to be able to begin each day with a commitment and intention to bestow that inalienable right to be loved toward those around us. We shall find comfort and strength together. Let us share this vision. Blessings always.

Chapter 3

Let's Play

The Role of Laughter

Angels can fly because they can take themselves lightly.

-G. K. Chesterton

Play is the language of the child within us all. As George Bernard Shaw said, "We do not stop playing because we are old, we grow old because we stop playing." According to Elizabeth Morey, a pastor in Syracuse, New York, who has incorporated many puppets into her sermons, "There is a child in every adult who would love to play if given half a chance. Puppets are wonderful bridges to the parts of ourselves we have forgotten or too often ignore."

The value of play is not a new concept. After all, it was Plato who said, "Life should be lived as play." Puppets are a powerful way of establishing rapport and connection with an individual. They also keep us connected to our creative, intuitive inner child.

However, while there are many reasons to introduce play, humor, and creativity to the persons you are working with, in a culture that prizes conformity, it takes courage to be yourself and innovate change. We often experience stress trying to live authentic lives, and the change might cause some anxiety and discomfort, but it is definitely worth the risk.

Smiles and Laughter Keep Our Light Shining

Do you remember Howdy Doody, Lamb Chop, Kukla and Ollie, Charlie McCarthy, and Jerry Mahoney? They were all puppets that made their audiences laugh – and laughter is powerful medicine for reducing stress, altering perspectives, eroding loneliness, and fostering hope.

A moment of lightheartedness in an otherwise dreary day is truly a gift. Laughter can help break the darkest mood and restore balance. People who can laugh at themselves tend to have a more positive outlook on life. When we laugh, we feel more hopeful and confident that we can handle the situation and can assume some control. In the many difficult and sensitive situations that arise in our lives, one of our best resources is laughter.

Laughter Erodes Loneliness and Provides Hope

Through laughter, we gain insight into our clients and we begin forming alliances with them. Humor and laughter help to communicate feelings and establish a connection. Laughter brings people together, eroding loneliness and promoting intimacy and communion.

Jacki Kwan, a clinical social worker and humor consultant in Maryland, knows the health benefits of positive humor and creativity. Jacki told me about a presentation she led for a group of stroke survivors when she used puppets. As she recounted, "Some of the people were in tears, so touched that someone would take the time to help them laugh. With tears in my eyes, I reached out and hugged one woman, in particular, who then asked if she could hug Snickers, the monkey puppet. I put Snickers' long, warm arms around her neck and the tears began to flow even harder. I knew, at that point, the power of these puppets in people's lives."

Mary Marstin from California is homebound and believes her puppets are her best medicine. She even suggests submitting claims for medical reimbursement for the cost of the puppets. For Mary, laughter is the cheapest and best medicine since it helps to alleviate both physical and emotional pain.

Laughter is contagious and helps to unite us with others. Laughter is universal, translates into any language, and transcends generations – it is not just kid stuff. My father was ninety-one years of age with Parkinson's disease and severe dementia. Nonetheless, he was blessed by an open, loving spirit and a great sense of humor that he was able to maintain throughout his entire journey through life. We often engaged him with fun-filled interactions at home with several of my puppets that readily opened him to play and connection to his beautifully, soulful inner child.

One summer evening, my husband and I took him to a comedy show; the comedienne had her audience roaring with laughter and my dad readily joined in with the rest of us. Although, he probably did not understand any of her jokes, for that one moment in time, he was the same as us, no longer different and isolated.

Humor in the Hospital

If one is disabled or infirm, one can easily feel helpless and powerless; laughter can break down barriers and help people see beyond their disabilities and illnesses.

Many patients and their families enter the hospital feeling fearful and anxious. Some patients fear they will not understand the jargon or the procedures, others assume there will be a lack of communication which erodes trust. Introducing humor and creativity into the situation can change perceptions, eliminate stress, and enhance communication between the health care provider and the patient. The result can be an increased level of trust and comfort, leaving the patient feeling empowered and confident to ask questions and become involved in the healing process. A puppet – a great addition to any humor campaign – can be used throughout the patient's treatment: during the interviewing or evaluation process, in the doctor's office, before anesthesia is administered, or as the nurse performs routine functions.

Patty Wooten, R.N., a clown and the author of Compassionate Humor and other books, notes that "patients with a keen sense of humor or playful spirit seem to have a strength and resilience which helps them weather the difficult and frightening moments of illness." Patty suggests that a sense of humor reminds us of the many blessings in our lives and provides hope and courage. She adds that "humor is a quality of perception that enables us to experience joy even when faced with adversity."

Many hospitals are dedicated to providing a welcoming setting that is warm, inviting, colorful, and friendly. Whimsical sculptures and paintings along with toys and puppets evoke smiles and laughter, helping to distract patients and visitors and diminish stress.

Bernie Siegel, M.D., celebrated author and presenter, adopted a white cat puppet from our Puppet Petting Zoo as a symbol of healing. He suggests that all emergency rooms should have puppets as an integral part of their environment. "Puppets help to distract the patient as they are powerful hypnotic and therapeutic tools," he says.

There are many props that can lighten the mood in a hospital setting. A "humor cart" can be introduced to inject energy and excitement into the day's routines. Special carts can be loaded with balloons, comic books, comedy videos, cartoons, kaleidoscopes, puppets, masks, and much more. A humor cart can add an element of intrigue and laughter. Patients' and visitors' spirits will improve and even the medical staff's stress level can be diminished as well. At Duke University's Comprehensive Cancer Center in Durham, North Carolina, the Laugh Mobile is nearly as common in the hospital corridors as the nurses' medication carts.

Clowns, Bed Pans, and Skunks

Shobhana Schwebke, M.A., of California, publishes the Hospital Clown Newsletter and is part of the Heart-to-Heart Caring Clowns, a group that is dedicated to uplifting hospital and nursing home environments with humor. "It's the little kindnesses of human warmth that touch the heart," she writes. "If we focus on our hearts and let our joy carry our work, that is the passion we will share with those around us. Too often we work out of obligation and responsibility. We focus on our time frames, managed care, finances, fatigue, and fear. When we focus on our heart, our passion, and extend our love and joy, it makes our work as light as the joy in our smiles and our hearts."

Shobhana works very closely with her puppets and has them with her at all times to break the tension. For example, she uses a skunk puppet named Flowers to help her and the patient get over the various unpleasant odors and sensory shock – bed pans and diarrhea accidents – that are common in hospital environments. Flowers lives in a bed pan on Shobhana's cart; its job is to shift the attention and embarrassment of both resident and clown so they can laugh with each other about the discomfort human beings share. Shobhana began clowning in the pediatric unit of an Oakland, California hospital because the administration believed that clowning was solely for kids. She writes: "It was just a matter of time before the hospital understood that clowns are for everyone!"

Humor Also Helps Medical Personnel

Humor is essential for staff, especially when life-and-death crises are a daily occurrence. It enhances their ability to cope with crises and tragedies. Laughter can reduce staff burnout, stress, and anxiety while, at the same time, providing comfort and hope to patients. It takes little effort and a limited budget to transform a gloomy and even negative environment into a more welcoming place for staff and patients.

Humor is a survival tool for health care professionals who do not want to lose their compassion and sense of caring. Lisa Rosenberg, Ph.D., R.N., studied the use of humor by emergency room staff and critical care units in 1995, and wrote: "There is a goodness of fit between how the provision of care induces stress in the emergency care environment and how the use of humor intervenes in that process. Emergency personnel experience a wide spectrum of serious events – trauma, life-threatening illness, chaotic emotional situations – often all at the same time. There is no time to emotionally prepare for these events, and little time to ventilate afterwards or 'decompress.' The spontaneous way in which humor can be produced in almost any situation, and its instantaneous stress-reducing effects, are well-suited to the emergency care experience."

At a therapeutic humor conference we both attended, Patty Wooten noted that we often have feelings of failure when our efforts are ineffective, when anger and frustration arise, when patients reject our care or are noncompliant with treatment or when patients die. "Caregivers," she added, "will often use humor as a means of maintaining some distance from the suffering and protecting themselves from a sympathetic response. We still express our compassion and caring, but without identifying with the patient's pain as if it were our own. Our ability to laugh provides us with a momentary release from the intensity of what otherwise might be overwhelming. We use humor to gain a new perspective and to find a way to function in a situation that could otherwise be intolerable. Laughter fills us with a joy which we radiate to others. It allows us to rise above our difficulties and experience the beauty of life beyond the hardships of giving care. We transcend our everyday problems and feel optimistic and hopeful."

Ann, a nurse in an emergency room in Massachusetts, experiences a lot of stress in her work environment. She has a little pair of Peepers – a pair of colorful eyes she slips on a finger, turning her hand into a puppet – and the simple, delightful creation has transformed her relationship with her patients. Her approach used to be rigid, but the playfulness of the puppet enabled her to free up her own feelings, thus softening her approach and helping her become more therapeutic in her interactions.

Easing Fears for the Young and Old

Being sick and receiving treatment in a hospital can be a frightening experience. The thought of upcoming surgery can be difficult for anyone to handle, particularly young children. A lack of understanding of what to expect can cause nightmares and distortions, which make the experience all the more difficult. Separation from the family during the hospital stay makes it even worse.

For scary medical procedures, a puppet can provide an immediate source of comfort and security for patients. Sara, a child-life specialist, discovered the comfort and security that a puppet can provide. One of her young patients was afraid of impending heart surgery. The girl would not let the doctor touch her and refused to talk. Sara introduced her turtle puppet and pretended that it would not come out of its shell, afraid that it would be hurt. Sara told the little girl she would administer each procedure to the turtle first, so that the child could observe.

If the turtle did fine, then maybe the child would too. An injection was given to the turtle with a real needle. When the child observed that the turtle survived the ordeal and was okay, she began to talk and cooperate with the medical staff. Over time, the turtle became the child's ally, offering support and security. Although it took some time for the child to learn to trust Sara and the puppet, it actually saved time for the physicians and hospital staff, since the little girl had been resistant and uncommunicative, preventing the necessary procedures from taking place at all.

Dr. Alex Kwan, an anesthesiologist in Washington, D.C., helped calm the fears of a three-year-old tonsillectomy patient by introducing "Doc," his monkey puppet dressed as a surgeon. "I saw her at the holding area," he told me. "She was crying hysterically and her mother was trying to console her. I approached them with 'Doc' and introduced myself as Dr. Kwan, the anesthesiologist, and Doc, my helper. The crying stopped! The little girl was looking at Doc with interest and I told her that Doc was very playful and has these extra long arms to give good hugs. At this point, I unfastened Doc's Velcro arms and gave Doc to the little girl to play with and hug. The child became calm and was now smiling at Doc."

Alex, Doc, and the girl's mother escorted the girl to the operating room where, with Doc in her arms, she was anesthetized via a mask. The surgical procedure was accomplished, and the patient was transferred to the recovery room where she woke up with Doc in her arms. "Her entire post-operative course was very benign," Dr. Kwan remembered. "She was not crying and, for the next three hours, she just dozed on and off until it was time to send her home. At this point, she became teary-eyed because she realized that Doc wasn't going home with her. Her mom talked to me about finding where she could buy another Doc because this was the only thing that made the surgical procedure go reasonably well."

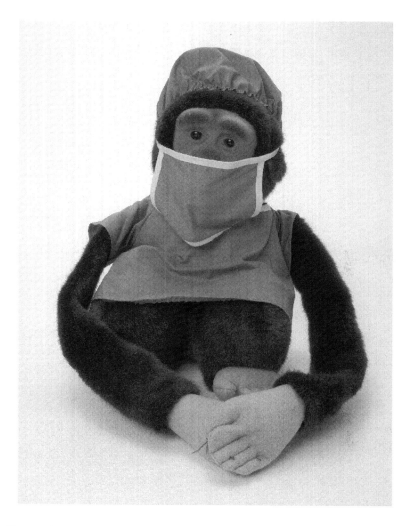

Dr. Kwan shared another story about Doc. A sixty-eight-year-old woman checked in for surgery for removal of a cataract in her left eye. As she was being interviewed by the admitting nurse, her nervousness and fear about her upcoming surgery were quite apparent. "I happened to be passing by and she immediately waved at me and said, 'Where is your monkey?' – referring to Doc, of course. Smiling, I told her that Doc was on vacation, but I would see what I could do about calling him in. I went back to my office and picked up Doc and gave the puppet to her to interact with. She was transformed from a scared lady to a smiling, composed patient. Surgery was performed, and she recovered and went home in a very good frame of mind."

Chapter 4

Your Magical Ally

Selecting The Right Puppet

Dream and give yourself permission to envision a YOU that you choose to be.

-Joy Page

With such a vast array of puppets available on the market, it's easy to feel overwhelmed when deciding which puppets to choose. Relax and have fun in the process. Although certain puppets will better serve people with different needs and at various levels of functioning, most people respond well to any puppet. The puppet you choose will be sure to bring laughter and joy wherever it goes and with whomever it interacts.

As you play and bond with puppets, if you feel fear and lack of confidence creeping in, try not to let that block your creativity. Understand that once a puppet is on your hand, the focus of attention is off you; you will not be judged as a puppeteer. When you put your hand in a puppet, you put your energy and spirit into the puppet; you bring it to life as an extension of yourself. A puppet is a reflection and animation of your spirit. What is vital is that you bond with and love the puppet you adopt. It is your loving energy that comes through the puppet which helps your client or patient in the healing process.

Considerations for Choosing a Puppet

The selection process is quite flexible; it really is up to you. For some people, the need determines the puppet. Others prefer to fall in love with a puppet first and then later decide how they can integrate it into their program. Sondra Hutchins, a nutritionist in South Carolina, prefers the latter way. She was drawn to two puppets at a conference I was exhibiting at: a red-haired little girl and an ostrich. She was unaware when she adopted them of how she would use them or of the grant money that would become available for their inclusion. She simply followed the attraction she felt for these two little characters while letting go of any specific goals, and an incredible program did evolve over time. (Sondra's work is profiled in Chapter 7.)

Considerations for choosing a puppet are: budget, size and type of puppet, comfort, size of audience, health concerns, whether it has a moving mouth, and the client's needs and situation. The cost ranges from just a couple of dollars for some of the little finger puppets, to thousands of dollars for custom-designed, life-size puppets designed by various artists. If funds are limited, keep in mind that sometimes the process of creating a puppet can be more fulfilling and therapeutic than purchasing one, as can be seen in the section below.

The size and type of your puppets is also dictated by the storage space you have. If space is limited, a wide variety of finger puppets is available. Finger puppets are tiny, making it easy to carry an interesting collection in your pocket, available for use anywhere and at any time.

Do you want your puppet to be realistic or whimsical? Are you going to need your puppet to be large enough for group presentations or are you mainly interested in working on a one-on-one basis?

Another important consideration is the wash-ability of the puppet. The vast majority of puppets on the market are surface washable. This means that you can take mild soap or Woolite and lightly wash the surface, without drenching the material. Then take a towel and rub it briskly, removing any excess water, and allow it to air dry. However, in certain settings, you might need a puppet that is machine washable and a smaller number of these are available. I suggest that you put your puppet in a pillowcase when machine washing and then tumble or air dry. If you machine wash a hand-washable puppet, the creature will most likely survive but the fur will change in texture and very likely become curly.

Do you want your puppet to have a moving mouth or would you rather it were silent? Sometimes it is essential that the puppet be able to speak, to help clients tell their stories or vent their emotions. However, some individuals may have a difficult time in opening up and sharing what they are experiencing, even through a puppet. In these situations, a puppet without a moving mouth might work better, since you can ask the person if the puppet can borrow his or her voice for a while, telling them that the puppet will give it back when they are ready. Moreover, you can suggest that the puppet will not divulge what has been shared, since its mouth cannot move, and that it will not reveal secrets to anyone. This can often be the catalyst for much enhanced communication. I consistently bring to life a rabbit puppet without a moving mouth when I work with aphasic individuals. Since a live rabbit is a creature of silence, I focus on its beauty in our world, not its words and the non-verbal ways to communicate.

Some people choose animal puppets because they are not gender-or race-specific; they also use parent and baby animal puppets for addressing issues of family dynamics. On the other hand, when using people puppets, there is a great deal of flexibility in the development of a character to fit a specific client's needs. People puppets cross all generations, cultures and disabilities; they are available in a variety of sizes and skin tones, can have specific characteristics of hair color, hairstyle, and eye color, and they can portray physical limitations as well. Outfits can be designed for additional identity recognition and bonding. However, collecting so wide a range of people puppets can become a financial drain.

A more economical alternative on the market is the "poly" or multi-use puppet along with an accessory kit. You start with a hairless base puppet (in any skin tone) that consists of a body from the waist up. Then, with commercial accessory kits, wigs, legs and outfits can be added on, turning the base puppet into any character you wish. You can save even more money by creating your own accessory kits.

Helen and the Grandmother Puppet

Most people respond with laughter and joy to virtually any puppet. But sometimes it takes a special kind of puppet to reach a certain individual. Helen, a ninety-year-old woman, was severely depressed after the death of her beloved husband of sixty-seven years. In my ongoing relationship with Helen, I tried to encourage a response with various animal puppets. The best I could elicit was a faint smile. I learned that Helen never had much of a fondness for animals and that they were never a part of her life. So I introduced her to an elderly female puppet. I was amazed by how this adorable two-foot-tall old woman puppet released Helen's warmth and affection. As I animated it, the puppet became a Jewish

grandmother, like Helen, with whom she could identify and whom she could immediately befriend. The puppet gave her the impetus to open up and talk, and that is what they did. Helen and the puppet talked about everything, from chicken soup to grandchildren. Helen admired how the little lady was dressed, shared how she enjoyed her company, and hoped she would come back and visit again. That grandmother puppet helped to fill a void, serving as a peer and friend.

The Fun Part of the Selection Process

When you decide what kind of puppets you need, do not forget the fun part – play! You need to touch, interact, and just have fun with your puppets. Some you will love right away, but eliminate any from your collection that you're not comfortable with. If the hand opening in the puppet is too tight, or the positioning of your hand is not comfortable, the puppet will end up sitting lifeless in the closet; your physical comfort is a significant criterion in the selection process.

Choosing the Best Puppet for the Issue

Individuals are unique, and so are their experiences and needs. Not everyone will respond to and bond with the same puppet. Certain puppets can best help you focus and address specific emotional issues and needs. Once you know which issues need to be addressed, it will be easier to decide which puppets can help bring about intended goals. Below are nearly a dozen different issues and the kinds of puppets that are most helpful.

Fear

Snakes, which hide in dark places, can help a client uncover hidden emotions and issues. As clients are helped to uncover and face their fears, they can better understand and deal with what they have kept buried. In this way, patients can more fully appreciate the parts of themselves that are open and well adjusted.

The caterpillar and other metamorphosing puppets are powerful tools in enabling the individual to express, understand, and work through fears of change, of the unknown, and of death and transformation. It is a universal symbol of change, of journeying from one state to another, and is very effective.

Additionally, a turtle puppet can aid those clients who are withdrawing in the face of an obstacle and are blocked by their fear. The turtle motivates them to stick their heads out and take a risk. A giraffe, too, symbolizes the strength and courage to reach higher and risk the consequences in order to achieve one's goal.

Separation Anxiety

A baby opossum attached to its mother's back or a joey inside its kangaroo mother's pouch can help address separation anxiety. I spoke to a mother of a three-year-old girl who had recently separated from her husband who illustrates this issue perfectly. After visiting with her father, the child was not able to verbalize her feelings. However, upon her return home, she needed to snuggle in bed with her mother with her kangaroo puppet in hand. "She loves the kangaroo puppet," says her mother, "because after a stressful event, the joey can get right into its mommy's pouch and mommy will take care of it and protect it." By role-playing with parent and baby puppets, children can work through their separation anxiety. By watching the child's interaction, you can gain insight into how he or she understands and copes with the circumstances at hand.

Inhibition, Withdrawal, and Boundary Issues

For an individual who is shy, fearful, or has difficulty verbalizing or making social connections, a puppet that can withdraw – either by moving its head in and out of its shell (such as a turtle, snail, or hermit crab), or that can roll up into a ball (a hedgehog or armadillo) – can be a way to express and connect. Often, not a word has to be uttered, yet the person will know that you understand his or her feelings.

Alice Miller, a clinical social worker, uses the turtle puppet for boundary issues. Clients often need to find a clear boundary or a protective, safe haven. The turtle does this by escaping into its shell, expressing the client's own need to withdraw. Of course, the client, particularly if he or she has been abused, ultimately needs to be able to come out of that shell.

Kathryn, a clinical social worker, guides her clients in establishing safe relationships through the use of animal puppets. When people in her therapy group are withdrawing, she passes them a hedgehog puppet. Its retreat, by rolling itself into a ball, helps her guide the group into discussing the withdrawal that she witnesses.

Anger

When clients need to vent their anger, a witch puppet, with its powerful and aggressive appearance, can help. A witch gives the client license to be furious, disruptive, and nasty, and then come to terms with what they are feeling and why.

There are many wild animal puppets, such as wolves, snakes, alligators, lions, and sharks that can help clients to identify and vent angry emotions. To reach clients who have been abused, who do not feel in control of their lives, or who have lost the ability to make choices, Carolyn Reeves, a professor of psychology and a private practitioner, chooses a puppet with a protective weapon. These include a shark's razor-like teeth, a skunk's odor, and a snake's venomous fangs.

Leslie, a group therapist, prefers a shark puppet when individuals in the group are being nasty to one another. She hands the shark to that particular individual and says, "That was a biting remark." She then helps them deal with their anger and frustration so they can learn to express their emotions in a less hurtful manner.

The "turtle technique" – using a turtle puppet that can withdraw into its shell – can be geared to those individuals who cannot contain their anger. When clients are feeling out of control, they can envision themselves as the turtle and pull back into their own shells. When clients begin to gain their composure, the turtle can begin to come out, little by little at its own pace.

Loneliness

A puppet that can best fill the void of loneliness is usually an animal familiar to the client, and of which the client has fond memories. A dog, cat, rabbit, or teddy bear tends to bring much joy, comfort, and security to patients, especially if the animal resembles one that the patient remembers well.

Harriet, a patient I worked with, lived in a nursing home. She loved her dog, Max, a golden retriever, and often spoke of him affectionately. Framed pictures of Max adorned her bureau and wall in her tiny room. Despite her open heart and alert mind, her eyes reflected a deep sadness and loneliness. But when I entered the room with my golden retriever puppet, she immediately perked up and her eyes twinkled. She quickly reached out for the puppet to hold it close and snuggle. There was immediate bonding and connection; in fact, I could have left the room and all would have been well. The comfort came from her connection to this puppet that elicited such fond and loving memories.

Accepting One's Dark Side

A witch puppet can help a client accept his dark side. Using a witch as mouthpiece, a client's darkest and most hidden thoughts can become heard, even acceptable, since the witch can take responsibility for what is said. A witch allows patients to be furious, disruptive, and nasty and then come to terms with what they are feeling and why.

Therapists working with women can use the witch puppet to focus on their dark side. Pairing a witch with a princess puppet, or an angel with a devil puppet, can make for effective alter egos, symbolizing the tension between light and dark, beautiful and ugly, positive and negative. A recreational therapist noted that she affixed a gold heart to her witch puppet to symbolize the beauty and richness of the inner being.

Jane, a clinical social worker in Connecticut, uses two witch puppets in couple's therapy – and with enormous success. She has the couple agree to exchange witches with each other. They are encouraged to act out the part of themselves that they keep private, their dark sides. Once they are brought out into the open, the issues can be dealt with. Jane believes it is only when we are willing and able to accept and understand each other's "witch" that we can begin to improve our relationships.

Vulnerability

Linda, a social worker, uses a wolf puppet to deal with issues of vulnerability. She depicts her wolf puppet as being very mean because it is afraid of being shot. Using this metaphor, her clients focus on their sense of vulnerability and the defenses that they use to cope with their own unique fears. Sometimes it is important for us to help our clients identify and analyze their feelings of vulnerability and lack of power. This type of analytical approach can be useful and certainly has its important place in the healing process.

At other times, we need to go beyond analysis so as not to dwell on the clients' despair. They do not always have to understand what is at the base of their behavior. With a lion puppet, patients can "fake it until they make it," roaring a roar that they really do not feel inside. Clients often mask their feelings of helplessness and vulnerability, and hide behind an enormous bravado, a giant roar. If they just keep roaring, maybe tomorrow they will feel the power that lies within them and that is inherently theirs. The lion puppet can also help to reveal the issues beneath that roar and help patients address why they are roaring so loudly while feeling so small and helpless within.

Self Esteem

Many clients face a loss of self-esteem as they age or battle an illness. They may be experiencing changes in their physical appearance and bodily functioning that diminish their sense of self-worth. The witch puppet, with its yellowing skin and less than beautiful features, can help clients deal with their issues of aging and self-esteem. Remove the witch's hat and put a scarf on her head, an apron around her black dress, and you turn the puppet into a kind old woman, a grandmotherly figure perhaps.

The beauty of the witch lies in her deeds and actions, not in how she looks. No matter how clients look, no matter what disabilities and illnesses they have, they still possess an inner strength and beauty – although they might need help to recognize it. Through laughter, creativity, and skillful intervention, patients can gain a more positive perspective and feelings of hope.

Because it changes from a mundane-looking caterpillar to a beautiful butterfly, a metamorphic caterpillar puppet can also address issues of self-esteem. Such a puppet is a striking metaphor for the beauty in us all. It can help clients witness and work through behavior that might be a result of trauma – a pressing need to crawl back into a cocoon – helping them discover the right moment to burst forth.

Aphasia

I bring to life a rabbit puppet when I work with people who cannot communicate verbally. A rabbit never utters a sound unless it is in danger. The puppet I typically animate is large, extremely soft and cuddly, and well represents the animal's gentle nature. I accentuate its beauty and sacredness despite its silence in the world, thereby helping the client to identify with his own beauty and strengths. One's external limitations do not diminish or extinguish the beauty of who we are. One's soul and spirit remain constant and ever present, easily identifiable and deserving of appreciation and honor.

Baby Puppets

Some people suffering from dementia are very vocal and talk profusely, although their speech is rarely clear or recognizable. Sherry, a client I worked with, often conversed with me enthusiastically, but I could not

understand what she was saying. Sherry readily connected and interacted with a variety of puppets, but on one particular day I brought out a baby puppet. "Oh, my gosh!" Sherry exclaimed joyously. She reached out to hold it. She clearly said the word "jump" as I made the puppet jump. On another occasion, Sherry took the puppet's hands to clap them together and uttered, "Look! Look! Look!" as if with pride at the baby's accomplishment. "Where is daddy?" Sherry questioned. "Is he working?" she asked. At the end of one visit, Sherry took the puppet's hand and waved it, repeating clearly, "Good-bye."

Angela and Mary were two of my nursing home clients, both of whom had severe dementia and who seemed to mostly live in their own worlds. When I brought out a baby puppet however, Angela readily engaged with it. She smiled, laughed, and maintained eye contact. Her words became clear and lucid. Angela questioned, "How old is she? Where's her mama? Where's her papa?" She remained attentive, focused, happy, and responsive. Angela was even able to appropriately repeat after me when I named some of the puppet's body parts.

As for Mary, when I brought the baby puppet to her she became playful and interactive. She held the baby, rocking and singing to it. "Are you having fun?" Mary asked it, adding to me, "Isn't it cute?" Usually, Mary seemed unaware of her husband's presence in the next bed, but with the puppet she clearly requested that I "show her to daddy," taking my hand and attempting to turn the baby towards her husband.

Maureen, in her eighties, was always neatly dressed and her hair fashionably coiffed. I frequently observed her touching her hair as if making certain of its neatness and was not surprised to learn she had been a beautician. Maureen appeared to be physically comfortable but often seemed emotionally stressed. As soon as I animated a baby puppet, however, Maureen gazed adoringly at it and reached out to hold and kiss it, smiling and quietly laughing. "You are the most beautiful baby I have ever seen; may God bless you," she said. On repeated visits, Maureen always noted how clean the baby's face, hands, and clothes were and kept repeating, "I love you." It was only during these interactions with the baby puppet that these women were able to maintain a continuous, fluid conversation.

Puppets as Metaphors

There are many puppets that serve as metaphors for a particular situation.

- **Eagle.** An eagle calls to all of us, "Look up, Climb, look beyond". The flight of an eagle symbolizes soaring to freedom and its keen eyesight can imply a clear vision and new perception. When we are burdened by trauma, grief, and pain, and are unwilling or unable to share our story, our wings become too heavy to fly, but the eagle puppet can help us envision a flight free of the troubles that hold us down.

- **Owl.** The owl depicts wisdom and it can see through darkness that others cannot. For those who feel vulnerable and helpless, an owl puppet can become their voice, their guide, their ally, and their hope. For Mary Keen of Florida who works with nurses in education and development, an owl puppet is really a symbol of the learning process, of being aware and alert, and developing a love of learning.

- **Octopus.** An octopus with its tentacles in motion can symbolize a client's hyperactivity and need to keep everything going at once. It can also represent the client's being overwhelmed and pulled in different directions at the same time.

- **Fox.** The fox is a quiet observer that is always watching. It may be useful with clients who have witnessed something significant and need encouragement to express what they have seen.

- **Ant.** An ant symbolizes diligence and hard work, but it can also stand for "Automatic Negative Thoughts" and can be introduced by a therapist whenever a client is in an unusually negative frame of mind.

- **Ostrich.** An ostrich can illustrate what happens when we ignore our problems, because when it buries its head in the sand, it is vulnerable to being kicked in the rear.

- **Bee.** A bee can be the "pollinator of possibility." One therapist I met uses it to encourage his clients to replace the old, negative stories of themselves with new positive ones filled with potential and hope.

- **Tadpole.** Because it transforms itself into a frog, the metamorphic tadpole shows how we are always changing and that our external appearance may not accurately reflect what we are feeling.

- **Baby Birds and Mother.** A mother bird, along with baby bird finger puppets, can help a client confront various issues, including abandonment, sibling rivalry, and the fear that there will never be enough love to go around.

- **Crocodile.** A crocodile can help clients address feelings of anger. Clients can choose to open the crocodile's mouth and let their feelings out, or they can keep the mouth closed with their angry feelings inside until they are ready to share them. This works especially well if you have a crocodile puppet with a mouth that opens and closes.

- **Dragon.** A dragon is used by many therapists to symbolize protection. For family counselors, the dragon can also symbolize a spouse who is "spitting fire."

- **Wizard.** A wizard, with its magical abilities, is an effective way to help clients reveal dreams and fantasies. It is a puppet of choice when using Steve Deshazer's "Solution Focus Therapy" for families and couples in which the therapist asks clients to describe the miracle they will experience when they awaken from a deep night of sleep.

- **Goldfish.** A goldfish in a fishbowl can symbolize a client who feels trapped and can only observe what is going on.

- **Clam.** A clam helps marriage and family counselors portray spouses who "clam up."

Another Option: Reversible Dolls

Although not puppets, reversible dolls possess interactive qualities that enable them to be used as therapeutic tools to promote self-discovery and healing. One example of a reversible doll is the "Wizard of Oz," which begins as Dorothy, and can be flipped over to reveal the Lion, the Tin Man and the Scarecrow. In times of pain and trauma, we might respond like the Lion, often unable to find our courage. At times we are like the Tin Man, unable to show the love we have inside. When we are overwhelmed by emotion, we might respond like the Scarecrow and lose our rational side. And, in a sense, we are all like Dorothy, on a journey home.

I met a real Dorothy, the granddaughter of Oz creator L. Frank Baum, at a conference on family therapy. She uses the Oz story therapeutically and travels the county to present her perspective on the dynamics of the Oz characters. She supports my interpretation and work.

Making Your Own Puppet

Donated, recycled, or low-cost materials are easily available and cost effective for making your own puppets. There are many books available about puppet creation.

I had the opportunity to create handmade puppets in my work with Robert, his wife, Sophia, and his eight-year-old grandson, Jack. Robert was 48 years old and was approaching the end of his life. He was tall, lean, exceedingly frail, and spent most of his time in bed. Once the sole provider and the grounding force of his small family, he was now struggling to keep his family together. Jack's father was in prison and his mother did not always make life decisions in her son's best interest and so Robert had become the boy's role model. Robert admitted to being fearful for the well-being of his wife, daughter, and grandson once he died and so tried holding on to every breath of life with determination. Sophia was unassertive and lacked confidence in her ability to survive on her own.

One day, after I had visited the family numerous times, Jack suggested that we make puppets. Sophia collected their old socks – Jack's preferred medium – and she had them ready for the next week when I brought an intriguing collection of art supplies. Robert rallied. He insisted on getting out of bed and began to create his puppet. Sophia also was enthusiastic about the project. "I'm an artist!" she proudly exclaimed as her puppet was nearing completion. They had so much fun interacting with each other and creating unique little characters that they all eagerly set about creating a second puppet. Robert remained alert and engaged for the entire time. Sophia felt so proud of her ability to create that it became a foundation for her future successes. The grandson was joyful and seemed to relish the intimacy that the creative process provided. Sophia found an elegant stand worthy to display all of their lovely creations: a legacy was created and, I trust, many cherished memories would continue to fill their hearts.

You are now ready to put your energy, your soul and spirit into the puppet and bring it to life. Please remember that the healing power of the puppet comes from *you*.

Chapter 5

Bringing a Puppet to Life

Animation Techniques

And above all, watch with glittering eyes the whole world around you because the greatest secrets are always hidden in the most unlikely places. Those who don't believe in magic will never find it.

-Roald Dahl

I meet many people who are inspired by the power and potential of a puppet but who have concerns about how to animate it. I have good news for you. If you lack the confidence but possess the enthusiasm and motivation to reach out and communicate with your clients with a puppet in hand, you will likely be your worst and only critic. There will be no external judges. A puppet is a manifestation of your spirit and once you animate it the focus will be off of you and directed to the puppet. The soul of the puppet is in your hand. It is your loving energy that will come through and help heal. While you are only limited by your creativity and imagination, here are some hints to help you get started.

How to Introduce Animal Puppets to a Client

Use caution when you introduce realistic animal puppets to your clients, as they might initially react with apprehension and fear. Start off standing at a safe distance until the individual reacts favorably to the puppet you're holding. When you sense a level of comfort, and the puppet is not perceived as threatening, step closer so that the puppet can be clearly seen. If there is no negative reaction at this point, allow the person to touch the hindquarters, keeping his hand away from the puppet's mouth and teeth. Additionally, the puppet's head can be bowed down and turned away from apprehensive patients. Once a comfortable, loving rapport develops, your creativity and sensitivity will take over.

If, at any point, the client expresses fear, discomfort, or lack of interest, do not force the issue. You might try backing off and saying, "I just wanted you to see my friend; we'll be back again another day." Always respect the person's decision and follow his lead. The next visit might be more promising, another puppet might be introduced with more success, or it may turn out that a puppet is not the tool you need to reach that person.

Whatever the case, the client's feelings and needs must be respected and met at all times.

Mastering the Movements to Convey Personality

Everything a puppet does should come from the personality of the character it represents. Movements should be distinctive for each puppet. Understandably, the keener your knowledge and appreciation of a particular animal species or human character, the more realistic your animation will be. Using simple and small gestures will enhance its lifelike qualities.

Mary Johnson, a delightful and talented puppeteer from California, created some of the most whimsical and endearing puppets I've owned and used. Mary believes that the movements you use to animate a puppet are more important than its voice. "Play with developing a character for your

puppet," she advises. "Learn to make eye contact between your puppet and the audience."

While developing a character might seem daunting if you're just getting started, the building blocks – movements that convey aliveness, physical attributes, and even personality – are not difficult to learn.

- **Breathing.** You can make your puppet breathe by simply moving your inside hand against the puppet's abdomen. You can wiggle the nose gently if the puppet is resting or quickly if the puppet is frightened. I combine a few simple movements to make my dog puppet pant. I open its mouth, allowing its tongue to stick out, and move the dog's head up and down slightly. Meanwhile, I make a panting sound, opening my own mouth and sticking out my tongue slightly.

- **Drinking and chewing.** For drinking, curl and uncurl your fingers in the puppet's mouth, causing the lips to simulate a sucking motion. If

the puppet does not have a mouth that can open, put a straw or cup against the puppet's mouth and move its face to simulate drinking. For puppets with a movable mouth, you can simulate chewing by using your hand to gently rotate the puppet's lower jaw in a circular motion.

Movements for Animal Puppets

Animals can have personalities, just like people, and there are movements you can use to create and convey the puppet's character without having to use words.

- **Shyness.** Have your puppet appear shy by slowly pulling your arm that is inside the puppet in to your body. Let the puppet peek out momentarily, then hide again. You can also cover the puppet's eyes with its paws. Hide the puppet's head in the crook of your elbow or against your neck. Have the puppet peek out and hide again.

- **Obeying commands.** You can have your animal puppet appear to obey your verbal commands. Tell your puppet to "sit" and then pull your arm that is inside the puppet abruptly back and slightly down. When you command your puppet to "lie down," flop the animal's chin down on your free arm.

- **Climbing.** If you want your puppet to climb, simply have the puppet run up your arm to your shoulder. Use your free hand to capture and pull the puppet down, then allow it to climb again.

- **Tail wagging.** To wag a puppet's tail, rest the puppet on your forearm. Put the thumb of your free hand over the tail, near the base, and stretch your index finger under the tail. Flick your index finger to move the tail. The frequency and speed of your movements should depend on which creature you are animating and whether you want it to seem relaxed or excited.

- **Paw cleaning.** If your animal puppet needs to clean its paws, have it use its tongue beginning close to the body, moving outward to the tip of the paw in a smooth, flowing gesture.

Movements for People Puppets

My main goal is to foster a connection – to transmit my loving energy to my client and help him to open up to his own story, his truth. The following tips can enhance your animation, which will help you create a believable character that your client can connect with.

- Try to make the movements and voice distinctive for each puppet character.

- No one will mind if you move your mouth as the puppet speaks. If you do not like the way this looks, another approach is to have your puppet whisper in your ear, allowing you to "translate" for the audience.

- Keep your eye on the puppet. There should be a split second pause between changes of idea; for example, turn (stop), speak (stop), wave (stop).

- Your puppet should stand erect and straight, with its fingertips slightly touching.

- When your puppet is talking to someone, keep it moving and have it look directly at the person.

- You can make the puppet seem more lifelike by having it appear to be aware of its surroundings. To do this, keep the puppet attentive by using your wrist to turn the puppet's head to watch what is going on nearby.

Matching the Movement to the Emotion

Some emotions and internal states can be conveyed with subtlety, while others require grander gestures. Simply bending your fingers can cause the puppet to nod its head in agreement and you can use your fingers to make your puppet tap or scratch its head to depict thinking; however, other emotions require bigger movements.

- **Laughter.** To have your puppet giggle or chuckle, use your inside fingers to bob the head. To move from a giggle to a laugh, use your wrist to have the puppet bend at its waist. To convey a big laugh, like a belly laugh, move your arm at the elbow to move the puppet's entire body. All of these movements can, of course, be coupled with the appropriate sounds.

- **Sadness.** You can convey whimpering or sniffling with the same finger movement used for giggling: bob the puppet's head while making the appropriate sound. Like laughter, the depth of sadness can be increased with bigger movements. You can use your wrist to bend the puppet at its waist and simulate crying; turn that into sobs of despair by moving the puppet's entire body with your arm.

- **Worrying.** With your wrist, move the puppet's head between its hands and have it sway from side to side.

- **Fainting or overcome with emotion.** Use your arm to make the puppet fall forward then backward, finally collapsing gracefully into a heap. To recover, use your arm to position the puppet first into a sitting position, from which it can rise slowly.

You do not have to spend a lot of time and energy practicing in front of a mirror to master the techniques in this chapter. Let the process be fun and allow your creative energy to flow.

Chapter 6

The Younger Generation

Eliciting Child and Adolescent Emotions

Wisdom begins in wonder.

–Socrates

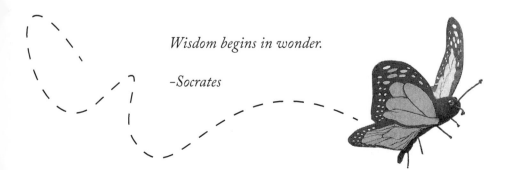

At a Child and Adolescent Psychiatry Conference I attended, I was touched by a story that one of the psychiatrists shared. She was working with a three and one-half year old little girl who was dealing with withdrawal issues. It was suspected by her family that her boundary issues had been sorely violated but she was unwilling or perhaps unable to process her experience and share it with her family. However, it had been several weeks and the psychiatrist was unable to elicit any information from the child as well. The psychiatrist began to notice however that each week the child was bringing her bunny puppet to the session and so she decided to question the bunny instead of the child. The psychiatrist was encouraged as the little girl slowly began to move the puppet until she was holding the bunny up to cover her face. The puppet became the safety net for the child as it was solely the bunny that was responding. She willingly permitted the bunny to tell her story of sexual abuse that had been committed by her uncle. This provided the necessary information required for the psychiatrist to move forward and eventually succeed in this man's arrest and help begin the child's process in healing.

Susan Everett, a supervisor of an expressive therapy department at a national acute-care psychiatric hospital for children, has helped children overcome extreme trauma, life-threatening depression, and other severe emotional distresses. Susan has a background in innovative and more traditional approaches to therapy and holds a masters degrees in creative expressive therapies and social work.

Several years ago, Susan Everett's nephew gave her a puppet sparking her interest in puppet therapy. "Puppets," she says, "make me the best therapist I can be."

In puppet therapy for children, the therapist gives young patients the freedom to express themselves but still serves as a guide, directing the child when necessary. Susan follows the child's lead; she has few restrictions or instructions, and this gives the child a sense of power and control in the self-exploration process. She trusts that the child's enthusiasm, creative energy, and imagination will help her to understand the situation. Her job is to get the conversation going in a dynamic way, keep it focused, and reframe and redirect it when necessary. As the puppets talk to each other, they become a bridge to communication.

A puppet forces adults to keep their language simple. Oftentimes a puppet will become a wonderful channel for unconscious feelings and thoughts. After venting and releasing her emotions, the child is able to pull back

and learn, understanding the connection between the situation and her feelings. Interacting with puppets helps to challenge the child to solve problems and maximizes the healing process.

In a group therapy session, Susan sometimes presents her puppet as having a particular problem. She then asks the group if any of them have been in such a situation. Or she might direct the conversation between the puppets around a particular theme, such as being in a hospital, or not being liked, or wanting to hurt oneself – and the participants perform a puppet show based on that theme. On occasion, Susan will have a puppet read a story with a therapeutic message; here, the puppet acts as the transitional object between the therapist and the child.

Susan usually sets out a wide variety of puppets and asks the children to pick the one that they are drawn to. The children's choice of puppets mirrors their feelings. When children are feeling vulnerable or scared, they often choose a puppet that can withdraw into its shell, such as a snail or turtle. After the children have chosen their puppets, Susan selects one, and the puppets talk with each other.

Susan also uses puppets to demonstrate and reinforce appropriate behavior. For example, for a hyperactive child who has trouble reining in his energy and who would run, jump, or bounce his way down the school corridors, she has had success using a long-legged marionette to model a slower pace and encourage the child to walk.

For teenagers, Susan sometimes holds teen-to-teen therapy sessions. One teen plays the therapist, and the other teen has some issues to talk about, trying to be as spontaneous as possible. As Susan notes, "They always seem to know, deep inside of themselves, what would be more constructive and healthy. Maybe they cannot apply it in their own lives at this time, but they know how to be understanding, knowledgeable and offer suggestions when placed in a leadership role with a puppet." If they have difficulty, Susan's puppet can help them refocus and become more positive.

Teenagers often reject puppets as childish. And yet, many professionals working with teenagers have found that they can be effectively reached through puppets. Eventually, puppets can actually get past a teenager's sophisticated attitude and lead to the trust and bonding so significant in the therapeutic relationship. When teens start to feel comfortable, they will use the puppets to tell the therapist about themselves and how they feel.

Using a puppet can create a distraction and help the teen to relax. As Kimberly Lauther Jackson, a child-life specialist finds, "Teens often have difficulty relaying information, which causes them to feel uncomfortable. Puppets can ease the difficulty which some teens have directly conversing about delicate subjects as well as being a creative outlet. Having a puppet express the issue allows the teen some distance from the subject without having to own it or confront it directly."

Kim further explains that having the puppet as an intermediary cushions the impact of what a teen says. Judgment or reaction is directed at the puppet, not the teen, allowing for the disclosure of difficult and sensitive information.

According to Kim, "For teenagers who worry about being accepted and struggle with their need for independence and the dependency that is necessary, particularly when they are ill, tools which enhance communication are vital to coping with [their] challenges.... Puppets may not be a comfortable tool for everyone, but should not be excluded from the possibilities for people over the age of twelve years."

Sam the Sarcastic

Kim tells the story of her discovery of how useful puppets could be with one of her older clients, Samantha, a challenging patient on the adolescent unit. Samantha, or "Sam," was hostile and unresponsive, fearful and withdrawn. One day, Kim entered, carrying an armful of materials for other patients. Within the pile was a frog puppet.

To Kim's surprise, Sam asked, "Who's that?"

"Oh, it's a frog puppet for Bob next door. He's younger than you and…"

Sam interrupted, "I asked, 'Who's that?' not 'Whose is it?' What's his name?"

Kim put the puppet on her hand and quickly answered, "It's Fips the Frog," Kim made Fips bow to Sam and extend his hand. "I am Fips the Frog, at your service, my lady. And your name is?" "I am Sam the Sarcastic," Sam replied, and a friendship was born. Kim had spontaneously created a character who allowed Sam a safe mode of expression and interaction. Sam the Sarcastic and Fips the Frog discussed Sam's fears and questions with the honesty and sensitivity of best friends and listened without making judgments. Sam and Fips remained friends for years, and Kim learned firsthand that puppets can be powerful tools for children of all ages.

David: A Teen's Love of Puppets

David, a teenage member of the Boston Area Guild of Puppetry and a budding puppeteer, was in an automobile accident and suffered a fractured skull. The first thing he did when he came out of a coma was to get his hand into one of his puppets. When asked how he was feeling, his puppet would comment on David's discomfort. While recovering in the hospital, he developed a friendship with a Russian child. Although a language barrier prevented them from conversing, they were able to communicate quite effectively through puppets. All of David's classmates made sock puppets for him to help speed his recovery. His mother commented on how amazing the gift was, considering how "un-cool" most young teens think puppets are.

Omar: Confronting Fears

At fifteen, Omar suffered from multiple sclerosis, was confined to a wheelchair, and was not given much time to live. Marie Roman, one of the social workers on my hospice team, tried working with Omar, but he was unable or unwilling to acknowledge and reflect upon his feelings. Marie encouraged him to accept a visit from me and my puppet family to no avail. Such a visit was not cool for a teenager. He kept refusing, and Marie kept inviting him to reconsider, suggesting that the puppets were beautiful and that if he did not like the first visit, there would be no pressure for another. Perhaps to get her off of his back, he eventually accepted. Omar, a handsome, intelligent, highly sensitive and gentle person, touched my heart from the moment I met him. I had learned from Marie that he loved dogs, and so I came prepared with every type of dog puppet I owned. Omar immediately engaged with the puppets, smiling and interacting with each one. He particularly bonded with the gentle breeds. We shared stories about each specific species. There was much laughter and playfulness, but the conversations always returned to the pit bull his father owned. We talked of our mutual fear of pit bulls. He seemed surprised and perhaps encouraged that I, a woman so much older than he, could have fears and be willing to express them. It is, after all, difficult to trust someone enough to admit vulnerability unless the other person can empathize and express their own. The key, of course, is that there can be no judgment. At the end of our session, I was pleased when Omar asked me to return with the dog puppets.

In time, he began to ask for the Rottweiler and German shepherd puppets exclusively, not the cute and gentle Labrador retriever puppies or the soft and lovable sheepdog puppet. He acknowledged some fear when he interacted with the rougher dogs, finding it hard to even pet them. Throughout the months that followed he asked for me to bring in a variety of other puppets, requesting wild cats, tarantulas, and snakes, sharing trivia about them that he had learned from watching many hours of television. He talked about his dreams of traveling the world – dreams he would never be able to realize – and expressed anger at the injustice of his situation. Then one day as we were interacting with the puppets, Omar said, "I'm more afraid of dying then I am of pit bulls." The recognition and expression of this truth led to an open and authentic dialogue about his fears, anger, and dreams. He then became fully open to cognitive therapy with Marie, although he never lost his loving affection for and connection to my gentle and lovable dog puppets and the visits that we enjoyed together.

Chapter 7

Young at Heart

Puppets in Long-Term Care

A friend is someone who knows the song in your heart and can sing it back to you when you've forgotten the words.

–unknown

Whether we serve elderly people as a professional or volunteer caregiver or as a caring friend or relative, it can be challenging to help them preserve their dignity and status and to maintain as much human contact as possible. We can use puppets to help these special people find security, ease, and joy, as well as a means of sharing their unique and compelling life stories.

In the world of puppetry, age is immaterial, as there is a child within each of us. Something magical often takes place when I introduce a puppet into the life of an elderly resident of a long-term-care facility. All of a sudden that individual has a new 'friend' to love and cuddle. This often leads to eye contact, smiles and laughter, and more interaction and touch.

While puppets do not work in all cases, I have seen countless examples where they have helped elderly people connect to their roots and interests and give expression to their needs and wants. In the three case studies below, with Bella, Frank, and Grace, you will see how puppets rekindled fond memories, elicited conversation and the sharing of stories and experiences, and helped to release repressed emotions. In the best cases, such as these, a puppet can help to create a new measure of comfort, tactile stimulation, and security in the person's life.

Bella: The Ballerinas

Bella, in her eighties, was mildly depressed, but cognitively alert. She was often soundly asleep in bed when I made my visits, and so for several weeks we did not have an opportunity to get to know each other. One day, however, Bella was awake and smiled as I approached her. I had known that Bella was a professional ballerina and that dancing had been her life's work. Now, however, she was hardly able to get out of bed. I hesitated to introduce her to my ballerina monkey puppet, feeling concerned that she might find it inappropriate or even insulting. I decided to take the risk, however, amazed and delighted at the magnetism I observed. This little dancing creature in its pink tutu and little sparkly hat fascinated Bella, and the intent gaze of the puppet's glass eyes impressed her. Smiling and laughing, she immediately reached out to hold the puppet, taking the monkey's long arms and wrapping them around her neck in a bond of friendship. She began to dance with her eyes and spirit, her face taking on a new vitality. Bella began to talk openly about her life and her three greatest sources of joy: dance, travel, and people. She named her new friend Moonbeam and began to "teach" the puppet some basic ballet steps as she moved its little feet. With great pride and warmth, Bella introduced her new protégé to her fellow residents and to the staff members who passed by her door. She found meaning and significance in the life she had lived, and I was able to reflect back the unique gifts that she had brought to the world.

Moonbeam inspired Bella to share her life story with me and gave her an effective and dramatic way to celebrate her aliveness.

Frank: Decreasing Stress

Sometimes the reaction to feelings of loneliness, frustration, and grief is not withdrawal but an explosive lashing out. Frank, a man in his seventies, was in the early stages of dementia. On the surface, he seemed affable, even gregarious. He initiated friendly interchanges with his fellow residents as if he were at a social club, attempting to organize an event or espousing a cause to other residents with dementia who could only gaze and sometimes even smile at him. Consequently, the staff of the nursing home was at a loss to understand his violent outbursts, including one day when he tried to throw a chair out the window.

The hospice team had learned that he had always loved dogs, and I was brought in to see if I could gather some insight into the root of his distress and to offer some calming and joyful interaction through the use of my puppets and music. Frank welcomed me every time I entered his room. He enjoyed my singing and he would, with a sheepish grin, often join in. He was mesmerized by the flute I played, attentive to its every note. He also opened to Reiki, meditation, and deep breathing exercises, which often helped when his anxiety increased. But it was the puppets that helped Frank to open up and enabled us to better understand his story.

Frank particularly connected with the dog puppets. He would hold them close, smiling broadly as he hugged each one and we talked about the various breeds. The physical interaction relaxed him, decreasing his stress and anxiety. He would come into the moment with a feeling of comfort, happiness, and vitality.

One day, when Frank was holding and petting one of the dog puppets, he began to weep in angry outbursts. The puppet triggered his emotional pain, ushering me into the secret dwelling place of those emotions. He talked about the death of his "best friend," a pit bull, which had been shot by a dog warden. Frustrated by his inability to right this perceived injustice, Frank wanted at the least to curse out the dog warden, but because of his dementia he could not even dial the correct phone number.

He later talked about other parts of his life over which he no longer had any control. Frank wanted to be in charge of his money, wanting the freedom to go to the bank and retrieve some of his funds so that he could spend it in ways, albeit small, that he found satisfying. On one occasion,

Frank's tender and kind offering genuinely touched me. He wanted to give me a financial gift so that I could continue my "good work." As he searched for money in his closet, he felt increasingly frustrated, demeaned by his inability even to find small change. Frank also felt angry about the quality of the facility's food and wanted to be able to get his favorite fast-food sandwich when he had an urge for one. He longed to go outside and get some fresh air in his own time frame, not the staff's, and to ride on his boat and go fishing. Frank was particularly angry at his adult daughter for putting him in the nursing home in the first place, and for what he considered her infrequent visits and unwillingness to take him to her home for the weekends. He felt vulnerable, angry, and distraught at his inability to change any aspect of his life.

I was touched by his ability to reach beyond his depression and confusion and articulate his pain with a purity and authenticity of emotion. Through the puppets, Frank had a comfortable and safe vehicle to express his anger and pain. I in turn was afforded the opportunity to respond with empathy to the truth about his world. Knowing what was bothering Frank, I could then attempt to remedy some of his problems.

Grace: Awakening from Silence

When we first attempt to interact with a person with diminished cognitive and expressive abilities, that individual might seem lifeless and empty. Grace, a tall, stately woman in her late seventies, is a perfect example of how you can still uncover an individual's spirit from beneath a seemingly vacant exterior. Grace had severe dementia and was restricted to using a wheelchair. She was nonverbal and unresponsive, looking out at the world with a distant and disconnected gaze as though she had retreated into a world of her own.

I had one important piece of information when I first began visiting Grace: I knew she had loved dogs throughout her life. So I brought every breed of dog puppet I owned with me to that first visit, hoping to spark some recognition or stir up an emotion. I sat close to her and brought each puppet to life, wagging its tail, suggesting that the dog was very happy to be with her and make a new friend. Each dog puppet nuzzled into her neck, licking her – sometimes audibly slurping her – and I consistently mentioned how the dog loved her. Nonetheless, her gaze remained distant and she seemed unaware of the puppets or of my presence. Despite her lack of response, I continued to visit her because she did not look agitated or afraid, no part of her body appeared to retreat or tense up, and her energy seemed to remain open and permitting.

On my third visit, as Grace was receiving a kiss from one of the dogs and I was again telling her how much the dog loved her, Grace clearly articulated, "Well, you've got to be good to them, you know!" That was the astonishing beginning to our new relationship. Suddenly, she began to vocalize and tell me stories. She often shared stories that perhaps were about her dogs as I was able to identify words such as "box" or "mess." Many of her words were unintelligible, but the fact that she was talking and communicating with another person was amazing and wonderful in its own right. She began to establish eye contact with the animated puppets and, in time, was able to transfer that eye contact to me. Unable to physically pet the dog by herself, she was responsive when I took her hand and placed it on the dog's fur to stroke. Visits became increasingly more interactive and fun. One day, Grace even clearly thanked me for visiting with her, but it was the puppets that allowed me to reach beyond the barrier of dementia and connect with her.

Whatever the patient's level of functioning, our challenge is to approach each individual with insight, sensitivity, and compassion so that we may connect with and best comprehend their thoughts, feelings, and needs. A puppet can be utilized as a conduit from our heart to theirs, a tool to open an avenue of communication.

Puppets for the Aged?

It used to be that puppets were not considered age-appropriate for adults and were associated solely with children's play. Until recently, although the introduction of puppets brought laughter, joy, and a general lightening of spirits for both the residents and staff of long-term-care facilities, the inclusion of puppets was prohibited. Acceptance of puppet therapy by the administrators of such facilities has been an uphill battle. Many an activity director had positive and encouraging interactions with their patients with puppet in hand but despite these consequences many administrators felt that it would be an insult to the dignity of their residents and would ultimately offend and anger their adult children. Today, however, many administrators agree that if an activity works for an individual and if positive outcomes and benefits are observed, then it should be considered an appropriate and useful therapy.

A few words of advice are in order for choosing puppets to use with the elderly. Rodent puppets, especially mice and rats, typically frighten elderly residents and are not a wise choice to bring into a facility. It is also best to avoid black or other dark colored puppets, since their features may be hard to distinguish by those with weak eyesight (a bright collar or bandana, however, can help to alleviate this problem). Still, if a dark-colored animal puppet is likely to spark recognition and possible connection it should still be used, as the story with Trista below well illustrates.

Trista: Licorice to the Rescue

No matter how cute and life-like a puppet might be, on occasion I do receive disapproving or doubtful looks and comments from people who do not comprehend the puppet's potential to help. Trista, initially,was one of those individuals. Trista was a hospice patient who suffered from severe depression. On my first visit, I brought a variety of puppets, hoping to spark some kind of response. Trista suggested that the puppets were cute and lifelike, but never once smiled and kept saying that her grandchildren would love them. "Why don't you just take them to the recreation director who could possibly connect you to a group of children," she told me. Seeing that my puppets were not reaching her and I was unable to evoke any joy or connection, I took myself off the case.

The following week I was quite surprised to get a call from a nurse on the hospice team informing me that my interaction with Trista had done everything she and her colleagues had hoped it would. Trista had been so negative and disengaged during my initial time with her that I wondered what she had seen that I had missed. The nurse told me that all Trista had talked about was one of my puppets, a little black Labrador retriever named Licorice.

When I returned, the facility nurse was in Trista's room and enthusiastically welcomed me, seeming relieved and grateful to see me. Trista seemed more open and receptive; her facial expression was less rigid and tense and her lips even gave the hint of a smile. She seemed comfortable and pleased to have Licorice there with me. Trista did not seem anxious to end the visit and never once suggested that I should instead take my puppets to a child. Then she reached into her night-table drawer and pulled out a group of photos, all images of a dog she had once owned and dearly loved – a black lab! Trista smiled freely, welcoming Licorice's attention and affection. Their connection inspired her to relate many happy memories from her past that she had not recalled for quite some time.

As the weeks went on, Trista began to anticipate our visits, even putting on jewelry and lipstick in anticipations of our time together. She took ownership of her part in the healing process, becoming increasingly involved and interactive in our sessions together. She eventually began to ask for what she wanted and requested that I sing songs from her Irish heritage. She began to accompany me willingly, sometimes even taking the lead. The joyful energy in the room was infectious, and Trista's roommate and her husband also found solace and joy by engaging with the puppets in lively interactions and joining in both laughter and song.

In the weeks that followed, Trista began to reflect on the root of her sadness, revealing stories of loneliness, grief, and emptiness. She told me that her relationship with her husband had not been loving and fulfilling and had caused her much pain. She was also saddened by the disconnection she experienced with some of her adult children who did not visit her often. At times, Trista felt very alone, but she would allow Licorice and me to fill some of the void in her life.

In time, I began to encourage Trista to look to the other relationships in her life that were loving and fulfilling and to open to gratitude for what she did have. She responded with disbelief when I noted how often her devoted sister visited her. She had taken this loving relationship for granted, ignoring its importance to her well-being, and began to awaken to its gift. In time, Trista's physical condition improved and she left hospice care. After many months of work, Trista was able to transfer the enjoyment that she derived from the puppets and music and join in the recreational activities offered in her facility. The last time I visited with Trista, she told me, "You brought sunshine into my life." She had transformed into a woman who could emerge from isolation and actively appreciate the world around her. We were both deeply grateful for the time we shared together and the impact we had on each other's lives.

Puppies or Puppets?

The therapeutic benefits of interacting with pets are well recognized and documented. Animals bring another dimension of caring that human beings cannot always bring to each other. An animal's unconditional love and acceptance can make a significant difference in an elderly person's life, augmenting the resident's sense of well-being, security, and joy.

A puppet therapy program can achieve many of the same results as an animal therapy program. These programs are not mutually exclusive; in fact, they can complement each other and are often effectively combined within the same facility. A realistic animal puppet can recreate much of the love and bonding that live animals elicit. Puppets can be a substitute for a real animal, whose comfort and connection residents long for, and can help those who are afraid of real animals to move beyond their fear.

The love that residents had for and the experiences they shared with their own pets make it likely that a dog or cat puppet, when brought to life with your animation, will help to initiate a spark of recognition that will promote interaction, connectedness, and joy. That is exactly what happened when I worked with Sally

Sally: A Bundle of Fur

When I first met her, although Sally was only in the early stages of dementia, other health problems had left her bedridden in a nursing home. Her affect was rather flat and her eyes looked dim and distant as I approached her bedside. I brought to life various puppets, but it was only when I animated a little tabby kitten that her interactions began to change. Sally readily welcomed the little bundle of fur into her arms. It reminded her of a kitten she once owned, and she briefly stared off into the distance, the memory alive in the twinkling of her eyes and a smile that brightened her face. She shared stories of her once-young children and their playful kitten. At each visit, Sally would ask to see my kitten puppet and as I animated it, stories began to emerge from her past about her relationship to her husband and the struggles she used to have with her controlling mother. On one occasion, she warmly advised me to live my life as I needed to, urging me to be authentic and honest in my life's experiences, suggesting that I could return at any time and she would gladly help me to feel better! It was such a tender reversal of roles. It illustrated for me the possibilities that can emerge when the puppet you choose to animate sparks a client's memories of a pet that once brought joy to their life.

Patient to Puppeteer: Finding Ways to Communicate

Many residents struggle to find acceptable ways to communicate how they feel. A puppet is a good starting point by acting as a conduit between the puppeteer and the resident. I have found that there are two equally valid approaches for encouraging communication; the one that is chosen will depend on what works best for the resident and what is most comfortable for the therapist.

One way to encourage communication is to place the puppet in the resident's hand and allow the resident to connect and interact with it. Often, clients are reluctant to share their feelings with others, but will open up to a puppet. Residents discover that the puppet is nonjudgmental and offers unconditional love. While bringing a puppet to life, residents can more easily discuss their needs, thoughts, and feelings. The resident is freed from responsibility for what the puppet says and words that might sound offensive from the resident's mouth are less so from the puppet's. However, when helping residents disclose their issues, the puppeteer cannot censor what the resident expresses. Of course, this first approach is not appropriate if the resident does not have sufficient mobility in the hands and wrists to move the puppet.

Another way to encourage communication is to have the puppet interact with the resident. Approach the resident with a puppet in your hand, allowing the puppet to express the emotions you have witnessed in that person. Have the puppet talk directly to the person and encourage a response. If you ask the resident questions and he chooses not to answer, consider asking the puppet. This way, the resident still has the option to interact with you indirectly through the puppet, but is not under pressure to do so. You will need to explore a variety of techniques, and many of those that are most effective are based not on hard guidelines but on intuition.

In the next two case studies, with Mary and Catherine, I used the second approach to successfully help both clients to communicate how they felt.

Mary: Connecting with an Unreachable Client

Mary was a client of mine in her eighties, confined to a wheelchair, and was assumed to have severe dementia. She would continually reach out her hand to staff or any passersby in the hallway as if wanting to make a connection of some kind. However, if anyone came close, she would pull at their sleeve or squeeze their hands so tightly that they would immediately withdraw and would think twice before approaching again. As a consequence of her often violent and abusive behavior, Mary rarely had sustainable connections or interactions and she was often left alone.

When I first encountered Mary, there were two student interns talking with each other at a safe distance from her bedside, certain that she was not able to comprehend their conversation. Mary was verbally unresponsive to any of my questions, turning away as if she had not heard the question or was perhaps incapable of understanding them. She would repeatedly slap her own face and occasionally let out a scream.

However, I sensed awareness on her part and what almost seemed to be a feisty spirit that echoed through a faint smile. I noticed a bright twinkle in her eyes that seemed to show that she was listening and comprehending my words. She remained focused as I spoke to her as if she was present in the moment and capable of understanding. I wondered if her rough behavior was really a crying out for connection. I left that first day excited and confident of a potential connection and was anxious to return the next week.

For several weeks, my puppets got little response from Mary. Eventually, however, a soft and cuddly kitten puppet opened a window to her heart and I saw the part of her that was warm, gentle, and loving. I worked at helping her accept the affection of the kitten, insisting that she herself was lovable and deserving of affection. At these times, I observed what I thought was a deep sadness in her eyes, but still no words were spoken. The kitten would nuzzle into Mary's neck, and I gently rubbed Mary's back and shoulders, and sang to her. During many of my visits, she continued to pull at my clothes and would sometimes squeeze my hand until it hurt. Each time, I reminded her that her behavior was unacceptable and that she did not need to force attention in that way.

I returned every week, kitten in hand. Mary began to trust that my visits were consistent, my heart open and accessible, and that I was present and receptive to whatever she wanted to share. It was clear that I had no agenda other than remaining firm in my unwillingness to allow her to hurt me.

After a while, Mary seemed to realize that she did not have to pull at my clothes and grip my hand to get attention. She began to get in touch with her pain and would sometimes cry. Only after weeks of interacting with my kitten and allowing herself to open to its acceptance and gentle affection did she begin to articulate the source of her pain: "I miss Mikey!" she cried. Mikey was her grandson, and because she was alienated from her son she did not get to see the boy. I was then able to help Mary focus on her part in this estrangement and her need to forgive herself and her son. I relayed this information to the social worker who worked at reuniting the family.

The kitten puppet helped to foster a connection with a nearly unreachable client and allowed me to help Mary find an acceptable way to communicate her feelings.

Catherine: Mirroring Emotion

Catherine, a small, thin woman with a flawless porcelain complexion was stuck in her bed. She was in her seventies, cognitively alert but choosing not to speak. Her body was contracted and her spirit seemed withdrawn; she slept much of the time. Catherine rarely established eye contact, but she seemed to listen, sometimes offering a slight nod of her head. She appeared uninterested in life around her and would not allow anyone into her private world. She was not interested in my puppets, turning away, and would sometimes fall asleep when I was with her. She seemed detached from life, as if she had given up.

I continued to visit her because, in time, she began to sleep less, kept her head turned in my direction, and maintained eye contact for longer periods of time. One day, I decided to mirror Catherine's body language with my turtle puppet. As the turtle's head pulled into its shell, Catherine, seemingly amused and surprised, was drawn to it. For the first time she broke into a broad smile and her eyes twinkled. It was as if a huge burden had been lifted from her. She looked beautiful and so much younger that I barely recognized her and was moved to tears. For the first time, she allowed me to open the blinds in her room and let in some sunlight.

I sat down at her bedside and asked why she was so sad. After much encouragement and a long, focused gaze of silent communication, Catherine chose to trust me and shared her story with me, verbalizing the root of her pain. She told me that she was afraid of dying and did not want to leave her family. I was then able to help her to understand that her behavior was actually working against her. In her retreat and silence, she caused her family to visit less frequently because she refused to talk or connect with them. As a result, she was creating the very thing she feared. I helped Catherine to focus on the fact that she was fully alive until her last moment of breath and fully capable of creating memories.

As I left her room, three staff members entered for medical treatments. I was disheartened as I watched Catherine retreat into herself once again. I held a prayer in my heart that she would be able and willing to maintain her voice, spirit, and hope until our next meeting. When I returned the following week she was once again distant and withdrawn. With a hint of anger in her voice she said, "Nothing has changed." Those were her last words to me. I continued to visit, but Catherine remained unreachable. She no longer maintained eye contact and seemed to will me out of existence.

I eventually decided to empower her with the choice to decide if I was to continue to visit with her. I told her that I would only return if she found her voice, any expression to make her intention known. If nothing came forth I would honor her silence as her command. She remained silent and I never returned. I cannot explain what happened, why she had gone from silence to speech and then back to silence. However, I did learn that eventually Catherine did come out of her shell and begin to talk and make the most of her life, which was encouraging to learn. I believe that the turtle puppet was key to providing the initial opening between Catherine and me and a bridge to her eventual opening to the world around her.

Speaking Through Puppets

Illness, aging, and death are subjects that people typically find uncomfortable to discuss. A puppet can give a patient license to talk about those subjects. Having the puppet express feelings that are observed in residents can free them to recognize and confront what they are experiencing. Once the issues are brought out into the open, residents can openly explore and deal with them.

A puppet can also assume responsibility for people's shortcomings, thus letting them feel more at ease and less embarrassed. For example, a recreational therapist at an extended-care facility in Richmond, Virginia, encouraged a resident with Alzheimer's, who rarely communicated, to animate a puppet during a small group-therapy session. As it turned out, the resident was very much aware of her condition. She avoided conversation because she knew she frequently sounded confused. Through the puppet, this resident was able to express her fear and embarrassment. In fact, puppets quite often break down barriers that can confine the elderly to a world of silence. Many long-term-care professionals have told me about residents who had not communicated for years and had suddenly begun to talk.

Barbara: Connecting to Memories

During her more active years, Barbara owned many cats and dogs. Now, she suffered from dementia and always seemed sad, although she would readily interact with my many dog and cat puppets, immediately reaching out to hold each one close to her. Barbara wept as she held a puppet and was able to tell her story of loss and loneliness. I could not remedy her situation, but I was able to provide opportunities for Barbara to release some of the pain that she held tightly within her by giving her the opportunity to reminisce, sometimes even smile and laugh as she connected to her memories and shared her stories.

Soothing Residents with Alzheimer's and Dementia

Agitated residents with Alzheimer's disease and dementia can often be calmed and comforted by introducing a puppet into their routines. I witnessed this myself in the early 1990s when I presented one of the first puppetry workshops for the staff of a Connecticut nursing home. Many of the residents were also seated in the workshop area, and one of the women was highly agitated and talked frenetically in a high-pitched voice. I tried to respond to her distress by placing a soft, non-threatening kitten puppet in her hands. I was concerned that she might throw the puppet but was confident that at least no one would get hurt. However, that never happened. To my amazement, her entire demeanor was instantly transformed. Her voice lowered to a normal pitch, her irritability vanished, and for the entire hour she talked calmly and lovingly to this little kitten. Although her words were still unintelligible, while she held the puppet she was comforted and content.

Several years ago, my husband and I were interacting with a group of residents at another nursing home in Connecticut. One of the residents with dementia in the group had been admitted a couple of days prior to our visit. We were advised that he had made several attempts to escape the facility and was so belligerent that he had to be physically restrained in his chair. Nevertheless, he allowed us to give him a chipmunk puppet and even extended his hand so that he could animate the puppet himself. During the entire hour, he focused on the puppet he had brought to life and seemed truly proud to have done so. The puppet quickly became his ally and protector. When a staff member attempted to take the chipmunk off his hand, he used the puppet to gently attack the hand that was attempting to remove it. Cheryl, the facility's recreational therapist at the time, suggested with great sensitivity that this puppet might prove to be the most powerful tool in helping this man adjust to his new environment, and she adopted it for him.

If you are concerned about how to afford puppets for residents who could benefit from them, keep in mind that lack of funds need not be a deterrent. Puppets can be created from donated, recycled, or inexpensive materials, or they can sometimes be obtained from thrift shops and yard sales. There even may be several of them hibernating in your or your colleagues' closets.

Using People Puppets to Reflect Diversity

People puppets offer a unique way to capture the essence of the elderly person while still maintaining a presence that is non-threatening and lighthearted. People puppets come in a wide range of sizes, ages, and skin colors and can reflect your facility's unique residential population. People puppets can wear eyeglasses, hearing aids, and medical dressings; they can be bald, clean-shaven, or have mustaches and beards, and they can be modified to portray certain disabilities. Puppets reflecting this wide variety of characteristics can be used in individual or group therapy, as a powerful addition to an in-service training, or as a mascot for the entire facility. For example, a recreational therapist from New York City had me create an elderly woman puppet dressed in a colorful and stylish outfit with earrings and necklaces to capture the spirit of many of her female clients. The therapist later adopted an elderly man puppet dressed in sophisticated city attire. Another facility had me create an elderly woman puppet dressed in a conservative dress and hat – proper church attire – as many of the residents attended church regularly.

Jenny and Annie

Jenny, a wheelchair-bound Jewish woman in her nineties, was belligerent, depressed, and hardly ever spoke. I was asked to visit her at the Hebrew Home with the hope that I might establish a connection but I was having no success. One animal puppet after another failed to interest her. The facility staff expressed disappointment, confident that Jenny could be reached, and after each visit they begged me to try again the following week. Eventually, I noticed that Jenny leaned away ever so slightly from the animal puppets and I thought that she might be afraid of animals or perhaps had never had a loving connection with them.

So instead of an animal puppet at the next visit, I brought Annie, a cute little girl puppet with mounds of red, curly hair and a large smiling mouth. She was double-handed, which meant that I could put my hands into both of the puppet's sleeves, giving her the ability to reach out and touch, hug, or hold with her soft little puppet hands. Jenny made an instant connection with Annie. She beckoned Annie to come closer and gently placed her on her lap, holding the puppet for the entire time that we were together. On other visits, I opened Annie's mouth wide as she sang to Jenny. When I had Annie sing in Yiddish or Hebrew, Jenny would join in, smiling all the while as she remembered and enunciated every word.

With the puppet, Jenny was able to stay connected to her heart place, demonstrating a calm and loving contentment, remaining focused on whatever Annie was engaged in with a grandmotherly pride.

Training Employees

An elderly man or woman puppet can help create a fantastic employee in-service training. The puppet (reflecting the residents' ethnicity, if appropriate) can represent the residents as it talks to the staff about how best to address their issues. A puppet can help take the heat off the recreation director, who may need to do some sensitivity training for the staff. For example, Karma Dorn uses people puppets at her facility to help her staff gain insight into the residents' rights, expressing their frustrations and serving as their voice. At a National Association for Activity Professionals conference, I presented a workshop on puppetry with Jim Brennan, a former health-care consultant. One of the participants confided that many staff members at her facility seemed to be lacking sensitivity and respect, often calling the residents "Sweetie" or "Granny" or merely calling them "you." After the workshop, she was inspired to help educate and modify her staff's behavior using an elderly woman puppet.

Advocating for Residents

Puppets can become advocates for residents' rights. It may feel more comfortable and less threatening for residents to express their concerns, needs, and frustrations through a puppet than by talking directly to the staff. Responsibility for what is said is projected onto the puppet. On the flip side, a staff member can use the puppet to voice the concerns of the residents. This might prove intimidating to some residents who do not appreciate such assertiveness, but if an elderly man or woman puppet is used, the staff member acting as the puppeteer could successfully mirror

residents' issues and concerns. After all, a resident's concern might be something as minor as a staff member neglecting to close a door or curtain, or it could be that the resident is harboring hurt and resentment toward a staff member who they think has been rude or disrespectful. The puppet can voice the resident's protest and make the staff attentive to his or her needs.

Residents' Adult Children

It can be a stressful and traumatic time when adults place their parents in a nursing home. In some cases, adult children might find it difficult to express the emotions they are experiencing. A puppet can relieve the tension and help the resident feel safe, as well as provide an avenue of communication between parent and child. Puppets that represent the parent and the adult child can help a family work out their issues in a constructive and accepting way.

A social worker from a nursing home told me about a resident's son who was concerned that his father was not readily joining activities. The father, however, was not troubled and was assimilating at a pace that he found comfortable. The social worker used an elderly man puppet to share the resident's perspective. Through the puppet, the social worker explained how each resident adjusts at his or her own pace and that not joining activities did not necessarily mean that his father was unhappy. The son was able to hear this and accept his father's level of involvement.

Including Puppets When Visiting Residents

I recommend taking along a puppet during visits to residents to spark laughter, humor, and connection. As Jim Brennan suggests, "Go on a people visit, not a room visit, with a puppet in hand." On different days, you might share a different puppet to keep alive an element of surprise and playfulness.

I was privileged to lead a workshop with Judith Wood, a therapeutic recreation expert at a New York medical center. Judith found that many of the residents were very receptive to the soft and cuddly puppets. "Their eyes would open wide and smiles would come upon their faces as they were greeted by staff and puppet. This type of therapy also had a calming and relaxing effect on them. With that in mind, we created a 'sundowner's activity' for those residents who became restless and anxious at the end of the day," she said.

Their program extends to the residents with Alzheimer's disease and dementia as well as to alert residents, who benefit from having a good time and a good laugh. Judith says her visits "take away the loneliness for a short while and provide emotional support and the reassurance that they are not alone, that somebody cares enough to pay them a visit. The program offers many opportunities for residents to experience reality and recall, as well as offer sensory stimulation. It allows them a short trip to fantasy land and gives them a chance to explore their own imaginations with joy and laughter."

One of the puppets that Judith animates is a Doozy Bird, a colorful, whimsical, forty-inch marionette. The bird plops its head in residents' laps and peers dolefully into their eyes. Its name is Izzy: "Izzy what? Izzy fuzzy? Izzy blue? Izzy happy? Izzy sad?"

Paul Weinstein is a puppet therapist who works at a number of nursing homes in his city. (Although he is called a puppet therapist, Paul respects the boundaries of his therapeutic work and does not do psychotherapy.) Paul became involved with puppets over twenty years ago, almost by chance. He attended a party where he picked up a puppet and began to

interact with the crowd. He was amazed at how the adults remained involved for hours and at the connections he was able to make with the puppet. He decided that puppetry was going to become his work.

Paul told me that the residential clients he works with are often moved to tears because the puppet characters he uses – two brothers and a sister – remind them of relatives they long to see. The puppets also flirt with the residents and poke gentle and affectionate fun at life. Paul adds that the staff also benefits, and that he has noticed a lightening up at the entire facility as a result of these visits.

Brightening Routine Functions

Routine functions, such as distributing medication, are often anything but cheerful experiences. Introducing a puppet – even a little finger puppet kept in a nurse's pocket – can brighten up an otherwise ordinary situation, providing laughter for both patients and staff.

A favorite puppet can augment a physical therapy program and help motivate residents to exercise and move limbs, making the routines more fun. A finger puppet can be the perfect motivation for performing finger exercises and, similarly, a glove puppet can exercise the entire hand. Additionally, there are puppets in which the arms, head, and mouth all move, providing opportunities to exercise a resident's wrists and elbows.

Maryanne Skomsky, a recreational therapist from Pennsylvania, tells of a resident, in the late stages of Alzheimer's, who has bonded with a particular monkey puppet. His response is so keen and attentive that Maryanne is able to encourage the resident to follow along and exercise by making the monkey puppet dance.

Some residents do not always enjoy mealtimes (sometimes they are not hungry; sometimes they just dislike the menu). To help dispel some of this unhappiness, staff members can keep finger puppets in their apron pockets and bring them out when a situation calls for some lighthearted humor. An apple finger puppet with a worm inside can poke fun at make-believe rotten apples being delivered to the nursing home. A small raccoon puppet can pretend to get into the dining room garbage or a monkey puppet dressed as a chef can help serve meals.

As a nutritionist, Sondra Hutchins, who you may recall from the chapter on puppet selection, prioritizes the restorative feeding program at the nursing home she works at in South Carolina. "The entire staff is committed to maintaining body weight…making sure we are reaching optimum levels," she explains. Sondra identifies opportunities to intervene with residents. She works with the residents who have eating disorders caused by dementia or strokes. Her goal is to turn eating into fun.

Sondra keeps up her residents' weight with humor and a novel approach: a "Spoodle" cart. Annie, her girl puppet, and her ostrich, Spoodle, help

Sondra offer the food. Annie might sit in a resident's lap and appear to take some food or be the one to offer the food. Annie sometimes helps the residents make dietary decisions. Residents have responded to Sondra's puppets and are constantly requesting visits. "The quiet dignity, low-key approach in gaining trust through a whispering puppet is most rewarding and effective," she says. "And the joy in finding dignity and the magic of a smile is the most humbling of experiences." Sondra has been so successful in her creative approach with puppets that she is asked to conduct workshops with other professionals around the country.

Ginger Helps the Medicine Go Down

Rose lay in bed, her face solemn, her eyes anxious, waiting, as always, for her daughter's visit. Fortunately, she had connected with Ginger, my orange cat puppet, and there was never a time when I entered Rose's room that she did not smile and eagerly ask, "Did you bring Ginger?" She eagerly reached out to hold Ginger close to her. Her eyes softened, as did her facial expression, transforming into a look of contentment and security. Ginger did not take the place of her daughter, but the puppet helped to fill a void for the moment. The bond became a strong and sustaining one. With Ginger at her side, Rose's belligerence and negativity subsided, although not her physical discomfort and pain. Despite episodes of severe pain, Rose adamantly refused her medications. Yet, even with her own distress, she always expressed concern over Ginger's well-being. One day I decided to pretend that Ginger was also experiencing some pain. Rose expressed relief when, without a fight, Ginger readily and calmly opened its mouth and took the medicine. Mimicking the cat, Rose opened her mouth and willingly took her own medications. The nurses always expressed relief when Ginger and I came to visit, confident that on that day Rose would not only be nurtured and experience joy but would take her medicine and get relief from her pain.

Creating a Conversation Piece

I have met many residents who have felt self-conscious and isolated because of their need for a portable oxygen tank or wheelchair. Sometimes it helps to attach puppets to these devices, transforming what was perceived as a stigma into a conversation piece. One woman at a nursing home in West Hartford, Connecticut, was excited to share with us how much attention she received because of a monkey puppet wrapped around her wheelchair. It became an added member of the community. Another woman who loved butterflies had me affix Velcro to the back of my many butterfly puppets so that she could stick them on her wheelchair. The puppets fostered a cheery attitude among residents and staff. When used in this way, the puppets help to put people at ease and place the resident at the center of positive attention.

Group Activities: A Puppet Production

Group activities help to overcome feelings of isolation and loneliness that can be prevalent in a long-term-care setting. Creative expression is sometimes neglected in the aging population, although we know that elderly people are still capable of creativity, of enriching their own lives and the lives around them.

Through participation in a group effort, such as a puppet production, residents can acquire new skills, gain confidence and self-reliance, and take pride in their collective creative efforts. Feeling needed and useful promotes a sense of dignity and self-respect and improves quality of life. Residents can write the script for a production, brainstorm themes, and vote for their favorite ideas. A group effort incorporates skills and interests that might have been dormant. Art, music, sewing, and knitting or crocheting puppets and puppet outfits can all be part of the endeavor.

The puppet production is an undertaking that can be worked on and shared with staff, family, friends, and volunteers; it can even become a community-wide venture or involve students from nearby schools – bringing generations together as an added bonus. The extent of involvement is determined by staff availability, resources that are available, and residents' enthusiasm. Keep in mind that puppets need not be store-bought; repurposed and donated materials can help keep costs down.

Diane Kieffer, activities director at an assisted living facility in Tennessee, relates a story about a community production. It began when one of the residents received a mule puppet as a gift from her son. The woman was proud of the puppet and wanted Diane to use it in her activity program. One of the residents named the puppet Muley. A group of residents decided that Muley was not going to be stubborn like most mules, but was to be kind, gentle, fun-loving, and willing to help others. Diane then worked with the residents to write a story about Muley. "It was wonderful to hear the residents express their feelings and ideas," she says. "They were very pleased with their accomplishment."

Once a month, a small group of residents takes Muley to a nearby preschool to entertain the children. One resident reads the story, another animates the puppet, and the remaining residents enjoy watching the show with the children. "Muley easily holds the children's attention, and they love him," says Diane. "The residents really got a 'kick' out of seeing the children make such a fuss over Muley. Muley has promoted laughter, enthusiasm, creativity, pride, and love in our facility."

Incorporating puppets into group activities can supplement sensory stimulation programs, since residents observe how the puppets work, recall the sounds of specific animals, and stroke the puppets' soft fur. Recalling pets they once owned, life on a farm, or animals that inhabited the wild can help residents reinforce their cognitive skills as they interact with and learn from each other.

Sharing Stories

Judy Busch, a nationally acclaimed ventriloquist from Tolland, Connecticut, entertains nursing home residents with her true-to-life people puppets. Judy's goal is to help the residents feel good about their lives, and to realize that they are still part of the world and have a valuable contribution to make. As Judy explained, "It's okay to be who they are and have their values. Those values are still good and solid."

Judy's puppets reminisce about the old days: the one-room schoolhouse, the horse and buggy, the general store. One puppet, Daisy, will talk about the loss of her fiancé, and the audience will sometimes shed tears. On occasion Daisy might read a love letter written from her grandmother to her grandfather.

Judy tells of a resident who got up to dance and another resident who told her to sit down, telling her, "You're making a fool of yourself!" Daisy went over to both of them and talked about how she used to love to dance, but now her feet are wobbly "puppet feet." Daisy helped both residents deal with the issue of dignity – an issue with real emotional significance for most residents.

My husband and I entertained residents at nursing homes, assisted living centers, and adult day care facilities with our puppets, storytelling, and music. Our goal was to foster the sharing of stories and help residents feel respected and valued. We encouraged residents at all levels of functioning to attend, since they all can receive some benefit. Most of the residents have a great deal of fun and exhibit a heightened degree of alertness, responsiveness, and interaction. Those that are at a very low level of functioning still seem to benefit from the warmth, comfort, and security that a puppet can offer and seem to receive the message of love and respect.

On one occasion, a ninety-year-old woman in an independent-living facility in Massachusetts became very excited when she saw our Canada goose puppet. It sparked warm and special memories for her, and she eagerly shared many interesting stories. She later decided, with great delight, to give a goose puppet to her nephew and his wife, who now live on the very farm she revisits in her memory.

Spanning the Generations

Residents experience pride and delight if they can still enjoy their grandchildren's visits. When residents can share a puppet with their grandchildren, it means a great time is in store for everyone.

Members of the older population have too often been isolated from the young. Karen, a recreational therapist in New Jersey, says that it is important to span the generations. "We are having a lot of fun with our puppets. Children relate really well to them, so they are proving a great way to break down some of the myths surrounding aging." In fact, to help Karen in this goal, one of her puppets is an older woman dressed in a jogging outfit, complete with headband and sneakers. So much for stereotypes!

Humor Therapy

Lenore Vitrone, a professional artist and clown, finds that puppets are an excellent bridge into the world of laughter and creativity. She enjoys "breaking the social image of the elderly as a lonely, burdensome, and infirm population. Although these conditions exist, they seem to loom large over us and blot out the positives."

Dressed as a clown and with puppets in hand, Lenore has developed a humor therapy program through which she offers her creativity, love, compassion, and listening skills to residents. Her puppets are the focal point of her program: they sing, dance, and tell jokes. Lenore says she "sometimes returns home after six to eight intense hours in two nursing homes, visiting from 70 to 120 residents, so 'high' with energy that I feel giddy.… That 'high' I attribute to the flow of spiritual energy that comes from bouncing vibrations of love and laughter back and forth between the residents and the clown." Although some residents hesitate to take a balloon or interact with a puppet, Lenore simply says, "I'm here for the kid inside us," and they almost always nod, smile, and accept her.

One of her puppets is called Limber Louie (a puppet sibling of Izzy as shown on page 112). Despite the fact that it is a forty-inch, whimsical, neon-yellow marionette, the residents will often ask her if it is real. Kenny is the name for her raccoon puppet that has an internal spring mechanism that makes it seem more life-like. The residents take one look at this puppet and begin a conversation that virtually renders Lenore invisible. They ask the puppet questions, wait for a response, and then answer the question themselves. "Most know Kenny is not alive, yet choose to enter into that reality that allows them to know it's okay to pretend. And yet, it's not just pretending – it's entering into a place that is real for that moment, is accepted and feels good. It's a space free from worry, a space that's harder to find in the everyday world where practicality and logic rule."

Lenore has one major rule: never leave a puppet with residents. She thinks they may misunderstand and believe it is a gift. On one occasion, she broke tradition with a bedridden resident, who had a difficult time letting

Lenore and Kenny leave. Lenore had been with her for at least twenty minutes and needed to visit other residents. She left Kenny resting on the woman's chest and made her exit. When Lenore returned, the woman said, "Shhh, he's sleeping." On another occasion, a resident asked Kenny if Lenore had been feeding him well. The resident had been petting him and felt the interior spring, thinking it was his ribs. It is hard to imagine how a puppet could become more real than that!

Chapter 8

Closing the Circle

Healing in Hospice

*Just when the caterpillar thought the world was over
it became a butterfly.*

–unknown

Hospice serves the physical, emotional, and spiritual needs of those who are expected to have less than six months left to live. Skilled medical care, caring presence, compassionate listening, and love are the essential gifts that a hospice team shares with the dying and the grieving. This chapter is dedicated to those compassionate, committed people who are involved in hospice work and the family and friends of those who are dying or those grieving the loss of a loved one. The hospice team can include a wide range of skilled care providers: nurses and home health aides, social workers and bereavement specialists, spiritual care counselors, complementary therapists, and volunteers. For me, it was a profound, sacred experience and great privilege to be part of a hospice team and I learned so much from the work, my team and my patients.

In hospice we believe that patients are fully alive until the last moment of breath and, furthermore, that dying is a time of intense learning when we can reclaim our wisdom and return to what is most genuine and real for us. Death, in fact, may be seen as a reclaiming of our wholeness. Illness and impending death force people into an acute awareness of their vulnerability. Yet, through illness, people can come to know and accept themselves fully and tend to move into a more authentic relationship with those around them. In realizing that we are each "perfectly imperfect," those who are dying tend not to camouflage their true selves and typically no longer worry about judgment, condemnation, or winning approval.

Using Puppets for Expression and Healing

In bereavement counseling it is crucial to let the dying and bereaved discover their own truths. We provide clients with opportunities to express their emotions, share their stories, and receive validation and support. By introducing puppets we can further this important work and help clients reach into deep expressive places that are not always reached by traditional cognitive techniques. Puppets can help clients overcome and transcend fears of pain, illness, and death, and can provide profound opportunities for healing.

To best support expression and healing it is important to use puppets in an empathetic manner. Puppets make no demands and do not impose their beliefs. Puppets listen attentively and give their unconditional love, but do not give advice or try to fix things.

Laughter in Grief

Puppets can also be used to enhance a client's quality of life – regardless of whether the client is the one dying or grieving – and bring a measure of joy and laughter to their day. This begs the question: does laughter belong with grief? Is it appropriate to encourage a grieving or dying person to smile and laugh?

Allen Klein, MA, author of "The Healing Power of Humor", "The Courage to Laugh", and numerous other books, notes that the serious business "of death and dying is considered by many to be no laughing matter. However, the outstanding coping and communication qualities of humor make it a valuable tool at a time when coping is difficult and communication is at a standstill. Humor can be an important component in the dying process because it can help patients, families, and caregivers not only get through tough times but also provide power in a powerless situation."

Shobhana Schwebke, publisher of the Hospital Clown Newsletter, notes, "As caring clowns we are often confronted by death and suffering. When I am spontaneous, I can trust my heart to be appropriate." She puts it best by saying that, "A joyful, loving heart is never out of place among the dying, the suffering, or the grieving."

The Solace of a Hug

Soft and squeezable puppets seem to offer the solace of a hug, and even the simple presence of a puppet in a client's lap offers much-needed comfort. When clients need to pour forth their emotions or unfold their stories, a puppet can be there to help tell the story or to receive the projected feelings.

- In bed when I arrived, Esther was feeling agitated, fearful, and confused; nothing made sense to her. When I brought some puppets to life, she laughed and clearly appreciated their beauty. When she felt fearful and confused, my dog puppet licked her, the bear hugged her, and the kitten came alive in her hands. The puppets alleviated some of her stress. Feeling calmer, she began to identify and articulate the source of her fears. When I left, she summed it up by saying, "It was a very wonderful visit whether it made sense or not."

- A petite and frail African-American woman, Trudy, touched my heart with her enormous courage and spirit. A hospice patient, she was experiencing a great deal of discomfort from a medical procedure. I tried to draw her attention away from her pain by playing a melody on my Native American flute, and this helped her for a while. I had learned that Trudy loved cats, so I brought to life one of my kitten puppets and had it gently nuzzle her neck. Despite her distress and pain, Trudy was able to smile and relax. Before we knew it, the nurse had completed her procedure, and Trudy had survived the ordeal. As she continued to nestle the kitten, I sang some traditional gospel tunes; her face brightened with a smile and she uttered an enthusiastic "Amen!"

- Louise bonded with Licorice, my black Labrador retriever puppet. She commented on the joy she felt from the connection and said that she would always remember Licorice. However, Louise – who was not at all cognitively impaired – expressed concern that the dog might forget her. I assured her that once a dog loves a human, it does so forever. Licorice's black color also led Louise to recognize her prejudice toward people of color, and we discussed the issue over many sessions. She eventually realized that "only the essence of the spirit is what matters" and began to see her prejudice as based in her own feelings of inadequacy, having a need to be punished for her own imperfections and failings.

- Agnes was feisty but frail and forgetful. Although one of her sons visited every evening after work, Agnes never remembered his visits. She lamented, "My sons seldom come; they are busy with their own lives. There's nobody to love and take care of me." Agnes did open to the love of a teddy bear puppet and told me, "I haven't been loved like this in a long time." It seemed to fill a void and provide her with immense joy and comfort.

- A woman in her nineties, Anastasia's quiet reserve and proper and dignified manner remained intact. She was always perfectly groomed and busied herself with tidying up her room. She readily welcomed my visits and particularly bonded with the puppy and human baby puppets; they seemed to tap into the child within her. In the moments we shared, Anastasia appeared to allow the comfort and joy of the connection to fill her. However, beneath her smiles and quiet laughter, her eyes spoke to me of a deep, intense pain.

Anastasia's ability to bond and connect with the puppets eventually extended to a deepened trust and connection with me. She no longer needed to mask her emotions and allowed the tears to flow as she held the puppets. Her mask of bravery and stoicism lifted, and she spoke about the root of the intense grief and the despair she felt over the loss of her adult son and husband. Although no one could remedy her situation, I believe that, in telling her story, she achieved a degree of acceptance that allowed her to experience a genuine sense of gratitude for the life she had lived and to close her circle of life with a newfound measure of peace.

Darlene: Mother and Daughter Connection

When I met Darlene, she was actively dying. A beautiful woman in her eighties, she had a sweet and gentle disposition. The hospice team had suggested that there was a deep sadness that permeated the interactions between Darlene and her daughter who was always by her side, and I was brought in to bring a little joy and inner peace to both of them. They enjoyed the music I played, but it was when I brought the puppets to life that their laughter and joy filled the room. Darlene was enchanted by the puppets' realism and the connection she felt to them. As her daughter said, "I haven't seen my mother laugh for such a long time, and it feels so wonderful to reconnect and remember that joyful, fun-loving part of her being."

Mother and daughter shared memories of the dogs and cats they once had as pets. Seeing the puppets captivate her daughter and hearing her daughter laugh and sing, Darlene was no longer consumed with worry about her future well-being and gained hope that she would be all right. Her heavy spirit lifted as she grew confident that, with time, her daughter would be able to move forward in life without her. These intimate and joyful interactions helped her close her circle of life with an added sense of peace and acceptance.

Linda: Affirming Life

Linda, an activity professional from New York City, has experienced first-hand how puppets can uplift and give her hope. Linda houses forty puppets on a "puppet tree" in her kitchen. Several years ago, Linda was sitting in the kitchen with her mother-in-law, grieving the loss of her twenty-six year-old son. Though they felt somber, her mother-in-law began to animate one of the puppets. Their spirits were lifted as they began to interact with the puppets and laugh together. Linda even felt an emotional connection to her son's spirit. He had loved puppets, and it rekindled warm and loving memories of their interactions together. "It was life-affirming," Linda recalls.

Melinda: Honoring the Clown

Melinda, a woman with severe dementia who could no longer speak clearly, would often tear up with joy when I entered her room. Her husband Ted, who was always at her side, would usually read a magazine while Melinda rested in her wheelchair. When she opened her eyes I noticed that her gaze would seek out Ted's presence and then settle, as if with a sense of relief, on his gentle, handsome face. Ted and I often spoke of his deep sadness and concern that Melinda's condition was worsening, as was his own stamina and physical well-being, which caused him a great deal of fear and anxiety.

During our months together, I brought various puppets to life, but the one that elicited the most joy was the sheepdog, as it resembled one they had owned and loved. As I animated it, Melinda would become playful and responsive, perking up and smiling as she opened to its love and affection. She allowed the sheepdog to snuggle and lick her with affection, mumbling cheery-sounding words as if enjoying the interaction.

Ted eventually shared with me that he had joyful memories of when they had been clowns together, showing me photos of them dressed in their colorful outfits. I followed up on this revelation by bringing in my clown puppet to try and tap into those memories and enhance the joy and laughter between them. Melinda smiled as my clown puppet came to life, as if recognizing an old friend. As the clown began to sing, Melinda made it dance, with Ted happily joining in. In the presence of the puppet, Melinda was responsive and alert. On one occasion, when I inadvertently left the clown's red nose at home, Melinda immediately noticed its absence and communicated it to me through touch and sound. Thanks to the puppets, a great weight seemed to lift from Ted's shoulders for those brief moments in time, his grief and fear melting away. He and I sang some of their old songs, with Melinda listening, smiling broadly, and sometimes moving her head to the rhythm. As Ted gratefully noted, "I haven't seen my wife so happy in a year and a half. I'm so grateful for your visits. You make her day!"

James: An Aura of Peace and Contentment

James was a man in his sixties who was on the verge of dying. A brain tumor affected the clarity of his speech and his thought processes, and he spent most of his time either sleeping or crying. Since there were photos of his family and their dogs in his room, I brought my dog puppets. He readily connected with Licorice, my black Labrador retriever puppy. At first, I could not get past the tears but, in time, James began to let me into his world – a world filled with much love, many fears, and much grief.

James became a father in his later years, and his daughter, whom he doted on, was the center of his world. As James interacted with Licorice, he would get in touch with his love for his daughter and her dogs. The daughter had been married for several years, but she and her husband had not had any children. Instead, her pets were like James's grandchildren, and James said that he would even throw birthday parties for the dogs. Like a grandparent who yearns to know the gender of his still-unborn grandchild, James did not want to depart from this earth until he knew what kind of dog she was planning to have next. As he loved and interacted with Licorice, James shared his fear of the love being snatched away from him.

Despite the fact that his son-in-law was a loving husband, James thought that no one would be as attentive to his daughter as he was, and he doubted his daughter's ability to survive without him. I shared this information with the social worker on our hospice team who intervened and helped the daughter realize that she needed to assure her dad that although she would certainly miss him, she would be all right.

James became tightly bonded to Licorice. His roommate told me that this puppet was all James talked about. One day, I came to visit but James was asleep. I gently called his name, but he seemed unable to open his eyes. When I whispered that Licorice was with me, James' eyes remained closed, but he quietly smiled and his hand crept out from beneath the sheet, tenderly opening to Licorice's loving affection. I talked with the hospice nurse on the morning before James died and she asked if I could visit him. James was weak, frail, and silent as Licorice nuzzled close to his neck. James was unable to speak, but there seemed to be an aura of peace and contentment that washed over him and prepared him for a beautiful closing to his life.

Puppets as Emotional Barometers

I have sometimes had to deal with clients who have a distinct edge. They react in ways that can be difficult to deal with and I have had to chip away at their belligerent exteriors. In these cases the puppets have served as barometers of the patient's emotional state.

Mario: Softening the Edge

Mario was angry, disgruntled – even caustic at times. He was in his eighties, frail, and alone. My hope was to bring forth the gentleness and warmth that I often recognized in his eyes as well as in his behavior toward his roommate. I learned of his love of birds and cats and brought an array of such puppets on my weekly visits. For the first several weeks Mario seemed to hold back a smile as the puppets came to life. However, he remained attentive and focused, intermittently maintaining eye contact.

It was the cat puppets that acted as Mario's emotional barometer. When Mario was angry and resentful he refused to acknowledge them. I continued to honor Mario's noble side, the beauty and essence of his soul, and my cat puppets never let up in their loving attention. I urged him to let his love out and share it, encouraging him to pet the cat. I was always able to tell that he was more relaxed and happy when he allowed one of the cat puppets to rest with him. At those times he would smile subtly and even, on occasion, admit that he really liked them, petting them tenderly.

In time, Mario began to talk about the grief he felt when his beloved cat died. On one occasion, he allowed me to hold his hand. I suggested that he had a lot of love inside him and that he was fully alive to share that love and positively impact the world around him until his last moment of breath. He squeezed my hand tightly and kissed it repeatedly as he cried.

Mario's room had no evidence of loving memories. One day, he requested to have a picture taken of himself with the cat puppets and I was delighted to do so. Mario's story strengthens my belief that it is never too late to create loving connections and open to the love around you.

Isabel: Revealing Abuse

Isabel, a woman in her eighties with severe dementia, spent much of her time crying. While awake she was often angry and sarcastic, with sleep her only refuge from emotional anguish. For weeks Isabel refused to have anything to do with my puppets and claimed they disgusted her. Yet I kept visiting because she was receptive to my singing, flute playing, and Reiki. Despite her claim about hating the puppets, when Isabel was in a better place emotionally she admitted how beautiful she thought they were, attempting to suppress a smile. She especially enjoyed cuddling with the sheepdog puppet and petting its soft, luxurious coat.

Once, while holding the sheepdog, she started weeping and began to tell me how her stepfather had abused her. Feeling alone and vulnerable in the nursing home had triggered those same unhappy childhood feelings. Throughout her life, Isabel had used alcohol to numb her pain and had developed few other coping skills to deal with her emotions. Allowing herself to open to the warmth and affection of the puppet helped her to hear the small voice of the child within her. I tried to help her see that she was safe now and her stepfather was no longer a threat. I encouraged her to reach out to a staff member she trusted. This seemed to help, although there were still many days when I found her hiding under the covers, wanting to escape. Yet there were also many days when Isabel allowed love, humor, and connection to enter her world.

Anna and Butterscotch

In her eighties, Anna had dementia and lived in a nursing home. She feared people who did not share her religion, but connected with me because we shared the same one and she felt a sense of safety and security in my presence. I helped to calm her anxieties by singing Hebrew and Yiddish songs, playing the flute, and bringing to life Butterscotch, a yellow Labrador retriever puppet. At first she was afraid of the animal, but the more she trusted me the more affectionate she became with Butterscotch, eventually reaching a point when she proudly said, "I'm not afraid, I love him! What a beautiful dog." However, her fears did not go away entirely. When she felt agitated, Anna would not open to a connection with the puppet; instead, with a look of alarm she would whisper "shhhh" and insist that Butterscotch and I leave. Anna confided her concern that we would not be safe at her facility, and the more she connected with Butterscotch and me the more protective of us she became. Although she welcomed us warmly and joyfully, responding happily to Butterscotch and the songs and stories I shared, after a while she would insist that we leave – yet would still agree eagerly to a next visit. For Anna, Butterscotch served as an indicator of her fear, as well as of her courage and ability to cope.

Lightening the Spirit

Laughter not only helps to heal, but it is a great source of relief for me and helps to lighten the intensity of my work. I have been surprised and delighted on numerous occasions by seeing how clients under physical or emotional duress can still maintain a sense of humor and how laughter can help to bring us together. Occasionally, I have been inspired by a client with dementia who expresses something cute or funny, possessing an inherent insight or compassion. At these moments, the laughter that their observations helped to evoke lightened the intensity of the experience.

- Confined to bed, in pain, and at the onset of dementia, Mildred learned that one of my puppets was named Licorice, another Butterscotch, and a third Toasted Marshmallow. She keenly observed to me, "Can't get you out of the candy jar!"

- Betsy enjoyed watching my flower puppet come to life as I sang. One day, as I encouraged her to sing along, she replied, "If I sing, my voice would kill the flower."

- Janet became upset when I was animating my yellow Labrador retriever and singing the song, "How Much Is That Doggie in the Window?" She asked with real concern, "Are you going to give Butterscotch up for sale?" I assured her that it was only a song and that Butterscotch was a very special puppy and was not going to be sold. Pauline felt just as protective about Licorice, my black Lab, when I sang the same song. "Not this one!" she said. "You stay here. I'll keep you!" I found their concern both sweet and touching.

- John, I first assumed, was only joking when he said that he had left some of his lunch for my puppy and kitten puppets. However, he seemed to bring it up at each of my visits and I began to realize that he really did want to feed my puppet animals. One day, when I was animating a very large rabbit puppet and he could not find his leftover lunch, John laughingly said, "He must have eaten my lunch to get that big!"

- Bedridden and given to loud outbursts, Rose always welcomed a visit from Licorice. On one occasion, Rose took some ice cream out of her mouth to share with the puppet. "Why won't he eat it?" she asked, intent on nurturing this puppy that she held close. Later, while Licorice rested in her bed with my hand removed from the puppet, Rose gently slapped my hand away when I tried to bring Licorice to life, adamantly insisting that I let Licorice rest. She was annoyed at me for my apparent lack of consideration. I was touched and amused by her genuine compassion and protection of the sleeping pup.

Leaving a Legacy

Sometimes puppets become a person's legacy – what they leave behind for their family and friends. Rick is a hospital volunteer who visits patients accompanied by his goose puppet. He and his puppet once visited a despondent seven-year-old with leukemia and, to everyone's surprise, elicited the boy's first smile in years. The next morning, Rick returned to find that the child had died. He was devastated, but the nurse reassured him that he had provided the child with an opportunity for joy, which perhaps was what allowed the boy to close his circle of life with peace.

Regina Marscheider, founder of Spectrum Puppet Productions in Virginia, works with patients in a children's hospital. She talks about Mickey, a five-year-old boy with a tumor who had been hospitalized and connected to tubes since infancy. A bone-marrow transplant became an option, but a requirement for this procedure was that the child be responsive. Regina was called in with her puppets and videotaped their sessions. Mickey responded to the puppets; it was the only time in his life that he had played. In time, he became eligible for the procedure but, sadly, died one week before the transplant date. His mother says that the video of Mickey playing with Regina's puppets is her most treasured legacy.

Expressive Puppetry for Children

Hospice is not only for older patients, as many children also have life-limiting illnesses. Puppets help to stimulate discussion with these children about their situations. Most times kids do not mourn gloomily; their grief is usually noisy and lively. Fun activities, such as puppet play, can teach coping skills in a non-threatening way.

Puppets can be equally helpful for children who have lost a loved one. According to scholar and author Dr. Nancy Boyd Webb, "Play therapy is the method of choice for helping bereaved children express their feelings. Although children often have difficulty verbalizing feelings of all kinds, their reluctance is greatly magnified following a death. When we consider that many bereaved adults cannot find words for their sorrow, it is understandable that children are especially handicapped. Play serves as the natural outlet for children to express and process their varied feelings of grief, even when they cannot discuss their internal world."

Victoria: Empowering the Dancer

When I met her, Victoria was a beautiful, bright, and sensitive six-year-old. Recently paralyzed from the waist down by a virus, she was now confined to a wheelchair. Initially she was quiet and cautious with me, but with each passing week, she interacted more with the puppets, smiling and laughing all the while.

After one visit, Victoria requested that I bring both a cheetah and a horse puppet; revealing that she liked them because of how fast they could run. Building on her request, I also brought a palomino horse puppet that was in a prone position. I wove a story for Victoria, explaining that the palomino was paralyzed and that the cheetah and the other horse, while able to run fast, were not altogether happy with their lives. Although Victoria was only six, she seemed to understand that each animal yearned to be something it was not. I explained to her that even though the palomino sometimes felt sad, that it was the only one of the three animals that felt gratitude for what it did have and appreciation for what it still could do. Victoria named the palomino Vanilla Flower and developed a strong bond with it. With Vanilla Flower as inspiration, she gained the ability to focus on what was positive and joyful in her life and what she still was able to do.

Victoria also grew to love Long Neck, the giraffe puppet. I told Victoria that this giraffe loved to dance, but was often mocked for its unusually long legs and awkward dance movements. In fact, I explained, my whole gang of puppets had different ways of dancing. The frog leaped, the turtle lumbered along, the butterfly flitted about, and the snake slithered slowly on the floor. I suggested that Victoria too could still move and dance in her own way, and began spinning her around and around in her wheelchair. This brought joy to Victoria and tears to her watching parents' eyes as they witnessed her empowerment and unleashed freedom of creative expression.

Jane: A Spirit Unleashed

I witnessed the meaning of unconditional love, respect, and honoring in the home of Derek, a sixteen-year-old boy with cerebral palsy. He weighed around fifty pounds, with a handsome face, dark brown curly hair, and large brown eyes. Derek was paralyzed, tube-fed, and unable to speak intelligibly. When I visited, he sometimes seemed to enjoy my puppets and music, but he was mostly engaged by the television. His mother, however, noted that our interactions provided him with a calming energy that lasted for a couple of days.

I worked some to help Derek's younger sister process and cope with the situation. Since the focus of attention always was on her brother, she often experienced jealousy and anger. Jane, Derek's mother, enjoyed the fantasy and whimsy of each puppet and would often find a moment of joy and relaxation by joining in our interactive songs and stories.

I usually work with animal puppets, but one day I brought along a little boy puppet that resembled Derek with his big brown eyes and dark, curly hair. Jane fell in love with him immediately. She named him Nick and he became quite a character in Jane's hands: a feisty, exuberant teenager, filled with a joy for life despite his struggle with leukemia and his bout with a hip problem that she invented. Nick just needed to be a "regular guy." Jane would make outfits for Nick, give him a funky hairdo and sunglasses, and provide him with a feeding tube. On one occasion, Jane even wrapped Nick up in a blanket so that he would be protected from the cold when I took him home.

Nick became a friend to Derek as well. On a couple of occasions, Nick slept over – the only time, Jane remarked gratefully, that Derek had a friend sleep over. The puppet provided Jane with a special time to be herself and feel free, and she often expressed her gratitude for having so much fun. "When Derek dies, I don't know what I'll do without you," she told me. We began to explore the options open to her; one of which was to work with puppets and special needs children, a task that she had a special gift for. Nick took on such a life for Jane that she wanted him to attend Derek's funeral.

Leroy the Lion

Kim Logan, a clinical social worker and the director of a hospice program in Missouri, works with terminally and seriously ill children and bereaved youth. Kim has developed an effective approach for dealing with questions and conflicts that can arise with a student's classmates. After Kim interviews the child's parents and teacher, the child returns to the classroom, often with a pediatric nurse who can answer medical questions. Kim enters the classroom wearing neutral-colored clothes and sits on a chair with Leroy, a large lion puppet, on her lap. Once Leroy speaks, the attention is off of Kim and the puppet becomes real to the children. There is no script and the narrative is simple: the puppet speaks in the voice of a child. Throughout the 30-45 minute session, the puppet stays in character. Kim ends the session when the questions become repetitive.

Kim uses Leroy as her primary means of interaction. In the case of terminally or seriously ill children, the puppet has the same diagnosis as the child and the nurse will ask the questions. When the classmates pose questions, the child can answer or let Leroy respond. Without putting the child on the spot, the puppet closely mirrors the child's situation, educating, conveying information, dispelling myths, and allowing the children to address what can be too difficult or frightening to confront directly.

Kim moves Leroy's mouth in time with his words, has him make eye contact with the audience, and incorporates lifelike lion mannerisms. The following are some examples of Kim's work:

- *The Girl Who Lost Her Hair*. A second-grade girl lost her hair from treatments for leukemia. On her first day back at school she was skinny and bald and when the students had to line up they told her that she should be in the boys' line. The children also insisted that she use the boys' bathroom. It was traumatic, and she told her mother that she would not go back to school. Her parents contacted the Leukemia Society, and Kim was brought into the classroom – with Leroy and a nurse – the next day. Leroy told the students that he had leukemia and was losing his hair. The nurse talked about how difficult treatment was and what the girl had to go through. It came out that the children had actually thought the girl was a boy and had not been acting with meanness or cruelty.

- *The Boy Who Might Die*. A boy with end-stage heart disease reentered school with increased fatigue, functioning at low capacity, and having to wear an oxygen mask. The staff and students were afraid that he might die at school. Kim and Leroy came into the classroom with the nurse. Leroy wore an oxygen mask so that the children could see that it was not a scary thing and understand why the boy had to wear one. The nurse asked Leroy questions about how he felt coming back to school. Leroy responded, "When I went back to school, my good friend Jimmy tapped me on my shoulder and asked me if I was going to fall over and die." The puppet was able to casually bring up what was on everyone's mind. The nurse explained that it probably would not be a sudden event, but rather a gradual process in which his heart would grow increasingly weaker. The anxiety and fear in the classroom were replaced by understanding and compassion.

- *The Nature of Grief.* An elementary school girl had reentered school after losing her mother and sibling in a house fire. She was whooping it up on the playground when a classmate came up to her and pronounced, "You must not have loved your mother!" The girl, of course, was devastated. Kim was called in, and Leroy talked to the students about the realities of bereavement. "Sometimes I need to play hard," Leroy said. "I need to forget and keep some parts of my life normal. That does not mean I do not love and miss the person who died." Leroy helped the children understand that grief for a child is up and down, from being deeply sad to playing and having fun.

- *A Balanced Memory.* A boy reentered school after the death of his brother, and Kim was brought in to help his classmates understand what it meant to lose a loved one. Leroy mirrored the boy's situation and explained that he too had lost a sibling. "Did you really love your brother?" Leroy was asked. "Yes," Leroy responded, "but my brother was sometimes a pain. He broke my favorite toy." The bereaved boy became very excited and cried, "Just like me! My brother broke my favorite fire truck." Kim helped the children understand that those who have died did not lead perfect lives and that it helps to have a balanced memory.

In cases of pediatric hospice in which a child might not get well, the puppet makes it safer to introduce this difficult subject to the child's schoolmates. The students will often ask if the child is going to die and the nurse will typically respond, "Sometimes, if the prognosis is good, we do all the work that we possibly can and then cross our fingers and pray that all goes well. However, sometimes the prognosis is bad and after all of the good work that is done, it still fails and the child dies." Through the puppet, even this, the most difficult of topics, can be openly, truthfully, and tenderly discussed.

Lifetimes

I have often been called in when a client's children or grandchildren are having difficulty processing and coping with the imminent death of their loved one. In these cases, I encourage the entire family to tell their stories and support one another.

For children and their families, I created a program based on the wonderful book *Lifetimes: The Beautiful Way to Explain Death to Children* by Bryan Mellonie and Robert Ingpen. I incorporate all the puppets mentioned in the book into the program. I typically begin with the puppets that are recognized as pets and foster a dialogue about the animals the family has owned. I ask if any of their pets have died. I encourage the child to understand that no matter how much their family loved their pet, and no matter how skilled the veterinarian's care, the animal still died. Using the puppets, I tell the child that every living thing has a beginning, a middle – which we call "living" or "lifetime" – and an end. This holds true whether the creature is a tiny insect, a tree or flower, a fish or a bird. I then talk about people, and specifically the child's loved ones.

My assumption is that when we experience the death of a loved one we are pained by the injustice of the death. We feel we are being punished. I help children realize that every living thing dies and closes its circle of life. The only difference is the size of the circle created. I remind the child that we are all alive until our very last breath and that the dying person fully appreciates that child's loving presence and attention. I offer suggestions of what the child can do to help the loved one live the remainder of his or her life in peace, empowering the boy or girl to take a more active role. Finally, we close by talking about how memories do not die but remain forever in our hearts.

Choosing Puppets for a Hospice Setting

Puppets are now being used in many bereavement centers around the country. Various puppets can be used with the hospice client and family members. In fact, by providing a range of puppets, you will better meet the needs of clients through all stages of the hospice experience. Below are some specific types of puppets and how they have been used specifically in hospice.

An Emerging Spirit: The Metamorphic Caterpillar

In working through issues of death and dying, a metamorphic caterpillar puppet that transforms into a butterfly can be a very powerful therapeutic tool to work through issues of death and dying. It empowers the individual to express, understand, and work through fears of change, the unknown, death, and transformation. It is a catalyst in developing an open forum.

A pastor I am acquainted with tells how he witnessed a metamorphic caterpillar puppet "being used for a part of a memorial service of a dear friend and saw how effective a teaching tool it is."

I've heard several people describe the meaning they derive from a caterpillar's transformation into a butterfly. As one bereavement counselor describes it, "One's body is like a caterpillar that spins its cocoon. When it dies, the empty shell is left behind, and the butterfly is like the spirit that emerges." Penny, a former hospice volunteer, says that when her husband died, a friend told her about the process of transformation from a caterpillar to a beautiful butterfly. Penny reasoned that if caterpillars can metamorphose into beautiful butterflies, then we, as humans, can emerge as beautiful spirits when we die. The fact that we cannot see our loved ones and friends or communicate with them after the transformation – which we call death – does not necessarily mean that they cease to exist. She found this concept to be very comforting.

Wings of Hope: The Butterfly

A butterfly is a symbol of hope and – like all living creatures – its lifespan has a beginning and an end. The middle, which we call "living" or "lifetime," is relatively short. Despite its short life, the butterfly touches us with its beauty, gentleness, and grace, and we treasure its presence.

Its short life illustrates that the quality of our lives matters more than the number of our years, and so it is vital that we focus on the living we have left.

I successfully incorporated a butterfly puppet into my work with Bernard, who was actively dying, and his wife, who was always present at our sessions. They both derived hope and inspiration from the puppet. After Bernard's death, his wife's love for butterflies led her to plant a flower garden to attract the winged creatures, which provided her with feelings of hope, joy, and peace.

If you want to incorporate a butterfly puppet into your hospice work, you can choose from a wide variety on the market, from dainty finger puppets to large, gorgeous satin creations. They are relatively simple to create, allowing you to select from many wonderful fabrics if you want to make your own.

One Step at a Time: The Turtle

A turtle puppet can help clients who have erected a shell and retreated into their own world. The turtle, which escapes into its own shell, can mirror the client's withdrawal and perhaps motivate the person to stick out his or her own head. A registered nurse and bereavement facilitator in New Jersey, Doris has successfully used the turtle puppet when working with bereaved families. Through the puppet, she helps the family and friends realize that they can, in their grief, "peek out and retract" as a way of coping with their loss. She helps them realize that they do not have to take on the whole world at once but can peek out, retract until they feel more secure, and then peek out some more when they are ready and able.

Hope and Pride Camels

Karen Minton, a bereavement specialist at a hospice in the state of Washington, says that, "Allowing people to share their feelings about their loss and to tell their stories before others who can identify with their situations is an important part of the support group's activities." She uses Hope, a camel puppet with detachable pouches and baskets. Each participant is asked to take one of the bags and talk about the burden they have been carrying around in their grief. Then Karen reminds them that the burden will be transformed into a treasure if they just hold on to hope. Hope's partner is a camel named Pride, who cannot stand on his own feet and flops down to the floor. Karen points out that if grief is suppressed and loss not dealt with, then the person will eventually cave in like Pride.

Courage: The Eagle

As the eagle puppet soars overhead, its "wings of hope" are spread wide. When people suppress their grief and pain, or anger and fear, they become

so burdened by the load that they cannot fly. However, when clients are helped to tell their stories and have the courage to vent their emotions, the weight on their wings can lighten, helping them embark on a flight for hope, growth, and inner peace.

Not Enough to Go Around: Baby Birds

Using a nest of finger-puppet birds with a parent bird can help a young client work through issues of fear, vulnerability, and anger, especially if the child is grieving the loss of a parent. The puppets can surface concerns about what will happen with several siblings and only one parent: will there be enough food and love to go around? You can also try reversing roles by having the child animate the parent bird while you animate the babies.

I had great success using a nest of baby and parent bird puppets with Heather, an extremely bright, creative, and sensitive six-year-old trying to cope with the impending death of her twelve- year-old sister. Heather spent a great deal of time with the nest of birds. She had it fall out of an imaginary tree, killing the little birds. In Heather's scenario, the mother was traumatized and saddened by the death of her babies. Different questions surfaced as Heather's story unfolded. We talked about "good" and "bad" doctors and how it usually does not hurt to die. Heather also needed to understand what would happen at the funeral. We enacted a mock burial and repeated it with the bird and other puppets until she began to grasp what the situation meant for her.

Separation Anxiety: The Kangaroo and Raccoon

A client may experience overwhelming sadness, fear, and anxiety from the impending loss of a loved one or a lengthy separation. You can help the client deal with these feeling by using a kangaroo puppet with a joey finger puppet in its pouch. In imagined scenarios, the joey might not find a place in the pouch any longer or perhaps refuse to leave the pouch entirely. This playacting can foster discussion and understanding. For

Kathryn, a mentally challenged woman in her twenties, the death of her mother and geographic separation from a close friend happened at the same time. Kathryn had a difficult time processing and articulating her emotions. She remained closed, retreating into her private space, unwilling to be touched or to converse. She was not sleeping well, which concerned her father. I used an adult and a baby raccoon puppet to narrate the story of the *Kissing Hand*. The book tells the story of a young raccoon who did not want to go to school because it did not want to separate from its mother. The mother kisses its paw and encourages the child to hold that love in its heart when they are apart from each other. At my next visit Kathryn wanted to hear the story again and again and wanted to animate the puppets herself. I encouraged Kathryn to remember that her mother and friend would always have her in their hearts, and that she would always retain her love for them in hers. I gave her a heart sticker to help her remember the story after

the raccoon puppets and I had left. She placed the sticker on a card and I wrote, "Mama and Margaret love me always. They are always in my heart." Kathryn's father said that she looked at it often and that it helped to calm her. She began to sleep at nights and her mood brightened. On my last visit Kathryn shared her love and heightened spirit with me, throwing her arms around me and hugging me tightly.

The Spiritual Connection

So many choices of puppets, so unique and sacred a world of individuals – to be respected, honored, and cherished. With a puppet in hand, I have been able to connect to a person's soul and discover the wholeness and integrity of his or her spirit. In most cases, the variety of puppets opened us to a world of laughter and gentle playfulness; they loosened us up to relax in each other's presence and open our hearts to each other in an intimate and sacred connection. These unique and beautiful people have been able and willing to articulate their dreams, fears, joys, and grief and to grow in fullness, joy, and peace.

I am deeply grateful for the people with whom I had the privilege to work. They grounded me with the humanity and fullness of our connection. We were able to relax our self-judgments and accept each other as we are with no need to fix or change. More often than not, they chose to make peace with the life they had lived and live until their last moment of breath. They seemed to be able to honor my presence from a position of inner strength and dignity, opening to feelings of love, self-worth and joy. They returned my love with an extraordinary gift of their own, so pure and unconditional, which dramatically enriched my life and for which I feel so privileged and grateful. When I learned how to really listen and to really see, they lit up my world. Their blessings will continue to wash over me as they live forever in my heart.

About the Author

Marge Schneider has worked in long-term care and hospice and draws on two decades of experience as an educator, complementary therapist, and spiritual counselor. Marge created the first expressive puppetry program for adults in the United States at one of the largest hospices in Connecticut, helping clients with dementia and depression find their voices and tell their stories. As the first hospice program of its kind, her work was featured in magazines as well as radio and television programs. Additionally, Marge developed a program that helped children and their families cope with the challenges of death and dying and find some inner peace and healing.

Marge conducts hands-on workshops in expressive puppetry across the United States and Canada, helping caregivers develop heart-to-heart connections. Her presentations educate and inspire and have been enthusiastically received at local groups and national conferences by nursing home staff, educators, activity directors, therapists, bereavement counselors, child and adolescent psychiatrists, social workers, storytellers, and gerontologists. To learn about scheduling a workshop or presentation for your organization or event, please visit www.expressivepuppetry.com.

Made in the USA
San Bernardino, CA
11 January 2016